# Parakeets FOR DUMMIES®

## by Nikki Moustaki

WILEY

Wiley Publishing, Inc.

**Parakeets For Dummies®**

Published by
**Wiley Publishing, Inc.**
111 River St.
Hoboken, NJ 07030-5774
www.wiley.com

AUG 2011

Copyright © 2007 by Wiley Publishing, Inc., Indianapolis, Indiana

Published by Wiley Publishing, Inc., Indianapolis, Indiana

Published simultaneously in Canada

For general information on our other products and services or to obtain technical support, please contact our Customer Care Department within the U.S. at 877-762-2974, outside the U.S. at 317-572-3993, or fax 317-572-4002.

Wiley also publishes its books in a variety of electronic formats. Some content that appears in print may not be available in electronic books.

Library of Congress Control Number: available from publisher

ISBN: 978-0-470-12162-7

Manufactured in the United States of America

10  9  8  7

1B/RV/QT/QX/IN

**Publisher's Acknowledgements**

**Project Editor:** Elizabeth Kuball

**Acquisitions Editor:** Stacy Kennedy

**Technical Editor:** Becky Margison

**Composition Services:** Indianapolis Composition Services Department

**Cover Photo:** © GK Hart/Vikki Hart/The Image Bank/Getty Images

**Cartoon:** Rich Tennant, www.the5thwave.com

**About the Author**

Nikki Moustaki, M.A., M.F.A., is an Avian Care and Behavior Consultant and the author of several books on birds and bird behavior. She has kept and/or bred lovebirds, cockatiels, budgies (parakeets), lories, macaws, amazons, conures, finches, canaries, ringnecks, and brotergeris. She advocates responsible bird

# Table of Contents

# The 5th Wave

By Rich Tennant

"I think the parakeet's getting bored with the toys you bought him."

# Chapter 1

# Parakeets: More than Just Pretty, Whistling Birds

*In This Chapter*

▶ Understanding what a parakeet is

▶ Telling the difference between the English budgie and the American parakeet

▶ Discovering the life of a wild parakeet

M ost people remember having a parakeet when they were a kid, and most kids today either have one or want one. As a companion, the parakeet has it all. It's small enough for even the smallest apartment, is as affectionate as any lapdog, and can even talk. What more could you ask for?

## First Things First: Using This Book

*Parakeets For Dummies* is a book I wrote for people interested in parakeets — whether you're a parent buying this book for yourself or your child or you're a kid buying it for yourself using your hard-earned cash. Maybe you just bought a parakeet and need the essential scoop on getting set up, as well as general care information. Or you may already have a parakeet and you need a refresher on the best way to take care of your pet or want to understand it better. Perhaps you're ready for a new pet but aren't sure if a parakeet is right for you and yours. If any of the above describes you, keep on readin'.

This book is a reference, so you don't have to read it in order from start to finish. Begin with Chapter 4 if you need basic set-up information, flip to Chapter 6 if you're trying to learn parakeet-ese, or head to Chapter 2 if you're still on the fence about adding a parakeet to your family. (Although if you prefer to start at the beginning and read until you reach the back cover, you're welcome to do so. I'll never tell.)

As you read, keep an eye out for text in *italics,* which indicates a new term and a nearby definition — no need to spend time hunting through a glossary. And `monofont` points out Web addresses for additional information worth checking out. You'll also run into a few sidebars (the occasional gray box); although the information in the sidebars is good, it's not essential to the discussion at hand, so skip 'em if you want to.

While reading *Parakeets For Dummies,* be on the lookout for these icons, sprinkled here and there:

This icon flags tips and tricks that will help you be the best para-keet pal you can be.

This icon points out information that's so important you'll want to be sure to remember it.

This icon highlights information on things that could harm you or your parakeet.

This icon flags information that you can use to impress your friends with your amazing bird knowledge, but it isn't absolutely necessary, so don't feel the need to memorize it.

# *What Is a Parakeet?*

The word *parakeet* is a generic term for any smallish, slender bird in the parrot family that has a long, tapered tail. But when most people think "parakeet," they think of the small, brightly colored bird common to most pet shops and to almost everyone's childhood.

Parakeets are about 7 inches in length (with the English budgie at around 9 inches), and most of that length is taken up by the tail. It is found in large flocks in the grasslands of the Australian outback.

You may also hear it called the *shell parrot* or the *warbling grass parakeet,* but its most famous (and interesting) name is the *budgeri-gar,* an aboriginal word meaning "good to eat." (Just don't tell that to your new pet!)

---

# Where parakeets come from

Parakeets arrived in Europe around 1838, brought from Australia by British naturalist John Gould and his brother-in-law, Charles Coxen, who raised the first *clutch* (batch of babies). Europeans found that these birds were easy to breed, and wealthy people fell in love with them. They soon became popular in Germany, Belgium, France, and Holland.

A yellow mutation occurred in Belgium around 1875, leading to other color mutations, including olive, dark green, gray-green, and light yellow. Companion parakeets were simply green until around 1881 when a Dutch bird keeper found a blue chick hatched in the nest boxes. This blue bird was responsible for other mutations: cobalt, slate, gray, and violet.

The parakeet arrived in America around the late 1920s, but didn't take off until the 1950s. Today, there are over 70 accepted color mutations and variations, and many other colors yet to be recognized. Even so, the most common colors are the most popular: green, blue, yellow, and white.

---

# You Say Potato, I Say Po-tah-to: The American Parakeet versus the English Budgie

Though the American parakeet and the English budgie both got their start in Australia, the American parakeet is more similar to its wild cousin than the English budgie is. The English budgie is what hobbyists call an *exhibition bird,* because it is often shown in large budgie shows (kind of like dog shows, but for birds). It's nearly twice the size of the American parakeet, and it claims its English name because the British were the ones who bred it to be the size and shape it is today.

The English budgie is basically *domesticated,* which means that it has been bred to make it more "appealing" for bird owners. This kind of breeding is what humans have done with dogs for thousands of years. (Notice how the different dog breeds look so different from one another — it's hard to imagine that they all originated from a couple of species of wild dog.) Though no parrot is truly domesticated, the English budgie is close.

Though technically called the *budgie,* the terms *parakeet* and *budgie* are interchangeable (see Figure 1-1 for an illustration of the two varieties). Some people call the larger version of the parakeet the budgie and the smaller version the parakeet — but it really doesn't matter which term you use. For the purposes of this book, I refer to these little birds as *parakeets.*

## Size difference

The American parakeet is smaller, thinner and more streamlined than its British counterpart. The English show budgie is stately looking, with a full, prominent chest and forehead. Its eyes are barely evident and its beak is tucked into the feathers of its face. It is 8½ to 9½ inches long and the American is about 7 inches long.

**Figure 1-1:** The English budgie (left) and the American parakeet (right)

## Temperament

The American parakeet is feistier than the English budgie, and may be more active than its mellow cousin. Both birds are good companions. Whichever type you choose, you can tame the bird into a wonderful pal.

## Lifespan

Lifespan is where the big difference between the parakeet and the budgie is evident. The big English budgie lives about 7 to 8 years, and the American parakeet can live 14 years or more.

This lifespan difference is because, in developing the English budgie as it is today, a lot of inbreeding was done (*inbreeding* is breeding birds that are close relatives of one another). Inbreeding can result in *congenital problems* (birth defects), shortening the lifespan of the bird.

# The Anatomy of a Parakeet

Knowing the parts of your parakeet is a good idea. When you know your bird's anatomy, you can describe a problem to the veterinarian if you ever have to do so. You can also speak like an expert with other hobbyists. Here are the primary parts of your parakeet:

**Crown:** The crown is the top of the head.

**Nares (nostrils):** The nares are at the top of the beak.

**Cere:** The cere is the fleshy area above the beak that contains the nostrils. It becomes blue in mature male parakeets, and pink to brown in females. When parakeets are young, it's white to light pink.

**Beak:** The upper and lower *mandibles* (jaws) make up the parakeet's beak. The parakeet is classified as a *hookbill,* meaning that the beak is shaped like a hook and is perfect for cracking seeds.

**Ear:** Your parakeet has small flat holes for ears, and they're covered by thin feathers that protect the ear. This is why you can't see them.

**Eyes:** The parakeet's eyes are on either side of its head so that it can see a great deal around it. This is because the parakeet is a prey animal and needs to be on alert for predators. Parakeets, like many birds, have a third eyelid called a *nictitating membrane,* which is a thin, semitransparent lid that washes the eye like a squeegee and closes for protection.

**Throat:** The throat is just beneath the beak and extends to the breast.

**Nape:** The nape is the back of the neck.

**Shoulder:** The shoulder is at the top of the wing nearest the parakeet's back.

**Breast:** The breast is just below the throat.

**Foot:** Everything that most of us think of as a bird's leg is actually a bird's foot. That's why the "knee" appears to bend the wrong way — it's actually the bird's heel. The parakeet's foot is *zygodactyl,* meaning it has two toes in front and two in back, perfect for grasping and climbing.

**Vent:** The vent is where your bird eliminates. In a human, this would be a combined anus and urethra. Birds do not urinate.

**Primary feathers:** Parakeets have ten long primary wing feathers that aid in flight.

**Secondary feathers:** The secondary feathers on the wing occur after the primaries, closer to the body.

**Rump:** The rump is beneath the primary flight feathers on the parakeet's lower back.

**Mantle:** The mantle is the back of the parakeet.

**Crop:** The crop is a sac-like organ that's kind of like a "first stomach." It's where the food goes immediately after being swallowed and is located at the breast.

**Syrinx:** The syrinx is equivalent to vocal chords in humans. It allows parakeets to talk and vocalize when air is pushed through it.

# Chapter 2

# Is a Parakeet Your Perfect Companion?

*I*f you're trying to decide whether to bring a parakeet into your home, you've come to the right chapter. But don't worry — even if you already have a parakeet, this chapter has something for you. Here you'll figure out what to expect from a parakeet (from its bubbly personality to the dreaded messes it makes) and what your parakeet expects from you. I walk you through the challenges posed by children and other pets (whether birds or not). I also give you information on owning more than one parakeet and fill you in on breeding (and what you should consider before you do it).

## Knowing What to Expect from a Parakeet

As wonderful as they are, parakeets are still considered wild animals, just as are all companion parrots. Though parakeets are about as close as a bird comes to being domesticated (other than the canary), they still have their quirks. Knowing what to expect from your parakeet — from personality to lifespan — will only make your relationship with your bird stronger.

## A great personality

As with humans, each parakeet is an individual with its own individual personality. Some are sweet and affectionate, while others may always remain fearful or aggressive. What you get out of your parakeet depends a lot on what you put into it. In general, a kind, careful guardian can tame a parakeet into a loving companion.

If you buy two parakeets that look similar, you may worry that you'll never be able to tell them apart. After you get to know them, you'll see that they have personalities of their own, likes and dislikes, different mannerisms, and different aptitudes for talking and training.

## Noise and talking

If you require an absolutely quiet home, then parakeets are not the bird for you. You're never going to prevent noise. They chatter, sing, and even talk for a good part of the day, though they do have their quiet moments.

A healthy and happy parakeet is quite noisy. Beware the silent bird — he may not be feeling well.

Parakeets are excellent talkers. They can even out-talk some of the larger bird species. Parakeets can learn hundreds of words and phrases and say them clearly and interchangeably. *Cocks* (male birds) are more apt to talk earlier and more frequently, but *hens* (female birds) have been known to do their fare share as well.

## Companionship

One of the best reasons to get a parakeet is for companionship. Parakeets are affectionate companions and bond readily to any human who is patient and kind. Your parakeet may love to stand on your shoulder while you do your chores or watch television. He'll preen your eyebrows and sing into your ear.

If you want your parakeet to be an affectionate companion, devoted to you, keep just one — as long as you're able to pay a lot of attention to him. If you have less time to spend you're your bird, consider a pair. This way, your parakeets will keep themselves entertained and occupied, and you won't have to worry about your bird being home alone and pining for you.

## Mess and noise

Birds are messy — that's the bottom line. You'll definitely be walking on a crunchy floor, and perhaps even a bit of water to go with it after the parakeet has taken her bath. You may even find seeds growing out of your carpet if you're not a great housekeeper!

Even if you buy all the seed catching devices and all the hooded cups on the market, you're not going to prevent mess. Get used to it and love your bird all the more for being the imperfect creature that he is.

## A decade or more of life — if you take care of the bird

Unfortunately, most parakeets only live a few years in the average home due to improper care and feeding, neglect, and accidents. But with the proper care, a parakeet can live 12 to 15 years or more.

The larger English budgie, because of its specific breeding, only lives to be about 7 or 8 — and that's an old English budgie. I've heard of them living longer with exceptional care.

# Knowing What Your Parakeet Expects from You

Your parakeet relies on you for all his needs: proper housing, nutrition, playtime out of the cage, and safety. You're responsible for every aspect of his life. In the following sections, I let you know what your parakeet needs from you, but here's a short list of the basic things your parakeet needs:

- ✔ **A clean cage:** You need to clean your parakeet's cage every day. Once a week, you need to clean the cage and the surrounding area more thoroughly.

- ✔ **Water:** You need to offer your parakeet fresh water twice a day. If he hasn't drunk all the water you gave him the last time, throw out what's there and replace it, so that your parakeet always has a fresh water supply.

- ✔ **Food:** Offer and change fresh foods once a day. Just as with water, if your parakeet hasn't eaten all the food you gave him the day before, throw out the old food and replace it with new.

(*Note:* You should change the water twice a day, but you need to change the food only once a day.)

✔ **Playtime:** Your parakeet needs safe playtime out of the cage every day. Be sure to keep a close eye on your bird — and on your other pets — whenever your parakeet is out of his cage. Also, check your bird's cage and toys daily for wear and tear.

✔ **Attention to his health:** Your parakeet can't just fly out to the vet's office when he feels a little under the weather. You need to watch your bird closely for signs of illness and take him to the veterinarian if you suspect something is wrong or if your bird has an accident.

✔ **A safe home:** When you bring a parakeet into your home, you need to make sure it's a safe place for your bird to live. (See Chapter 4 for more information on parakeet-proofing your home.) Also make sure that your parakeet's cage is away from drafts and that the room where he lives doesn't get too cold or too warm.

In addition to these basics of bird care, your parakeet needs other things from you, covered in the following sections.

## A good home

Parakeets need as large of a cage as your space and budget can afford. If you can't buy a large cage, then save up until you can. A cramped parakeet will be quite unhappy.

A parakeet's environment needs good lighting. It can be indirect natural lighting with some direct sunlight during the day (though the bird should have a shady spot where it can retreat). Or, you can use special bird lamps, which you can get at the pet shop. A spotlight and a special bird bulb should do the trick. Birds need sunlight or full spectrum lighting to be healthy.

Ideally, the temperature in your parakeet's environment should be between 70° F and 85° F (21° C and 29° C). Make sure that your bird doesn't get too cold or too warm, and that it has clean, fresh water at all times in hot weather. If your home is below 70° F (21° C) at night, make sure to cover the cage to keep in the heat and keep out drafts.

Before bringing your parakeet home, make a space for his cage in an area where he's bound to get the most attention. I like to place my companion birds' cages in an area where they can see me most of the time, like in the family room. They get the added bonus of being able to watch television (and believe me, they like it!).Your parakeet is *unlikely* to get a lot of attention in a garage, child's room, or patio.

## Time

Expect to spend at least two hours a day with your bird. You should spend more time with your parakeet on the days when you have more time — but two hours is the bare minimum. That's a commitment of at least 14 hours a week, possibly more.

Cleaning, feeding, watering, and playing with your parakeet all take time. You'll also spend time making arrangements for her when you go away on vacation and you'll spend time in the veterinarian's office.

If you're thinking, "Oh, she's exaggerating — I'll be able to take care of my parakeet in fewer hours than that," you may want to ask yourself why you want the bird in the first place. Spending time with your parakeet — even doing the not-so-fun things like cage cleaning — should be something you enjoy, not something you try to get out of. If you're looking for ways to avoid it, that may be a sign that a parakeet isn't for you.

## Routine

In the wild, parakeets schedule their day around the sun. They understand the seasons and how to behave when water or food is scarce or plentiful. In nature, the same events happen day after day, year after year, and these birds are programmed to go with the flow.

Create a routine and try to stick with it. Your bird should know exactly when you're going to feed him, when you're going to clean his cage, when he's coming out for playtime, and when it's time for bed. If you keep a routine with your parakeet, he will eventually alert *you* when you've missed a step. If your life is hectic, just do the best you can.

# Deciding Whether a Parakeet Is Right for You

If you're still not sure whether a parakeet is right for you, thinking about who you're getting the bird for (yourself or someone else, like your son or daughter), how much money you'll need to spend taking care of the bird, and what kind of home you can provide is a good place to start. Parakeets bring joy and happiness into millions of homes, and your bird can bring the same to yours if you've thought seriously about what you'll need to give.

## Vacationing without your bird

Some people don't think about things like vacations when they buy an animal. Try to recruit a responsible friend, neighbor, or loved one who will take care of your parakeet when you're away. If you can't find anyone, call your local veterinarian or pet shop and inquire about boarding there.

If you're away from home more often than you're there, you may want to think twice about getting a parakeet. Parakeets are great companions — which means that they like your companionship as much as you like theirs.

## *Looking at why you're getting the bird*

If you're an adult and you want a parakeet for yourself, you're off to a good start. Parakeets are not just for children, and they're not starter birds. A parakeet and adults can have a wonderful relationship — as can parakeets and children.

Here are some good reasons to buy a parakeet:

- ✔ You've always wanted a parakeet.
- ✔ You've had your eye on a particular parakeet in the pet shop and you've fallen in love with him.
- ✔ Your child wants a parakeet very badly and you (the parent) are willing to assume full responsibility of the bird.
- ✔ You had parakeets as a child, you loved them, and you want to have one again.

Some not-so-good reasons to buy a parakeet include the following:

- ✔ You need something to match the drapes.
- ✔ You want a bird and a parakeet is all you can afford.
- ✔ You want a pet for your child that's not going to live very long.
- ✔ Your other parakeet died of some disease (you didn't take him to the veterinarian) and you need a replacement bird.

If you're buying a parakeet for a child, realize that *you* may be the one who ends up taking care of the bird, even if the child promises to feed him and water him and clean him and play with him and love him everyday. Though your child may have the best of intentions, more often than not, the parent assumes responsibility for the animal.

Parakeets *can* provide a child with a sense of responsibility, compassion, and companionship. The qualities that a child learns from caring for a bird are qualities that he or she will use for a lifetime. Children who have parakeets learn to love, care for, respect, and maintain another being — and that valuable hands-on lesson lasts well into adulthood (see Figure 2-1). Having a parakeet will also teach the important lesson everyone has to learn eventually — that nothing lives forever.

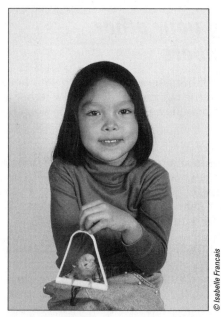

© Isabelle Francais

**Figure 2-1:** Kids and parakeets can make great companions.

Even if the parakeet is the child's bird, place the cage in a room where the bird will get attention from the whole family. Explain to the child that the bird will be lonely in the child's bedroom because she is away most of the day. If the child is gentle and handles the bird well, you can allow her to play with the bird in her room. Problem solved. (See Chapter 6 for more information on helping your children to handle a parakeet safely.)

## Knowing how much it will cost

All the parakeet accessories that you'll need to get started — like a proper cage, cups, toys, and a play-gym — can take a chunk out of your wallet. A parakeet can cost anywhere from $10 to $25 for an American parakeet, or $45 to $100 or more for an English budgie.

Then there are trips to the avian veterinarian for well-bird checkups, which you should do yearly. When your avian veterinarian gets to know your bird, he or she will be better able to take care of your bird in the event of an accident.

Parakeets cost around $15 per month in food and accessories. You may want to splurge now and then on extra toys or treats, which will bring the total expense higher.

## Considering your other family members

If you're thinking about bringing a parakeet into your home, you owe it to the parakeet and the current residents — whether animals or humans — to think about how everyone will (or won't) get along.

### Children

Parakeets should not be allowed around babies. Parakeets often carry diseases that are communicable to people with under-developed immune systems, which include babies. Though toddlers have a stronger immunity, they may not understand that they have to be gentle with such a fragile bird.

Even kids that are a little bit older can harm the bird when the parent isn't looking. The child can let the bird out of the cage, try to catch it, or feed it something harmful. When you get a parakeet for a child (or have a child in the home), make sure that the child is mature enough to understand this animal's needs, and be sure to supervise your child's contact with the bird.

### Dogs and cats

Dogs and cats are *predators* and parakeets are *prey*. What this means is that your loving Fido or Fluffy will want to kill and eat your parakeet — hard to believe but true.

Cats are fascinated by small, moving objects, which basically sums up the total of your parakeet's being. To top that off, cats have a type of bacteria on their claws and teeth that is deadly to birds. So if your cat even nicks your parakeet with one little claw, your parakeet is in trouble. Never, ever, *ever* allow your cat access to your parakeet.

Some dogs, like terriers, are bred to chase small, fast-moving objects. Other dogs, like spaniels, poodles, and retrievers, are actually bred to hunt and retrieve birds. Other types of breeds are content to not think of your parakeet as a meal but as toy, and this is not a good scenario either.

If you have a big dog, be sure that your parakeet can't get to his water dish — these little birds have been known to drown in dog and cat bowls. What a sad way to die.

### Other birds

People often keep parakeets in aviaries with other birds. I've seen parakeets living peacefully with cockatiels, canaries, and finches. *Remember:* You need a lot of space in order for all these birds to get along.

Some birds can be quite vicious and dangerous to your parakeet. Lovebirds, for example, will not tolerate any other birds in their vicinity. A larger parrot may also take offense at your parakeet's presence and easily kill your little parakeet.

# The "pity" purchase

Sometimes buying a bird that looks very ill is tempting. Perhaps he's the most plucked, sorriest looking parakeet of the bunch. He looks like he's going to keel over any second. You know the bird I'm talking about — the one who's hearing the angels singing already.

This bird is not only going to cost you a fortune in veterinary bills, he may infect your other birds with whatever he has, and the pet store is just going to buy another sorry bird to put in his place. You're always better off sticking with healthy birds from the beginning.

If you feel really sorry for the parakeets in a particular pet store, you aren't obligated to go into that pet store anymore — and for goodness' sake, don't buy birds there. You can call your local Humane Society and hope that something gets done about the conditions in the store. You may want to call the store's owner as well — that usually works for a time.

Before you bring another bird home to your old birds, you must set up a place where you can *quarantine* (isolate) the new bird. This place should be well away from your other birds, and you should care for the new bird last and wash yourself after each interaction. Quarantine traditionally lasts 40 days, though some people quarantine only for 30 days.

### Other pets: Ferrets and fishes and snakes, oh my!

Other pets in the household can also pose a threat to your small parakeets. Snakes are a major enemy for birds, and a snake is savvy enough to figure out how to get inside your parakeet's cage and eat him whole. Never let your snake loose around your bird. Ferrets and rats will also stalk and kill your parakeet if allowed near the cage.

Fish tanks also pose a danger to your parakeet if he decides to take a bath in the "pretty lake." Drowning is a major cause of death in birds, so be sure to keep your fish tank tightly covered.

# One, Two — or More: Increasing Your Parakeet Population

If you want a sweet parakeet that lives for seeing you come home every day, a parakeet who is so enamored with you that you can barely move without him stuck to you like a burr, you'll want to have one — and only one — parakeet. If you get a pair of parakeets, they may want to interact only with each other, seeing you as an intrusion in their birdy love.

On the other hand, if you lead a busy life and you're not home for many hours of the day, you may want to consider getting a pair.

Just because you have a pair, or more, does not mean that your parakeets will not become hand-tamed or won't love you, but you may have to work a little harder to get them to see you as one of the gang.

A single parakeet, especially a single male, is more likely to talk. This doesn't mean that birds in a pair won't ever talk; it just means that the likelihood of getting them to talk is lessened the more parakeets you have.

## Looking a gift parakeet in the beak

Giving a parakeet as a gift isn't a great idea. You may think that you're giving a *parakeet,* but what you're really giving is a 15-year sentence with a bird that the person may not like — and vice versa. Take into consideration that the person may have wanted to choose the parakeet on his own. Maybe you got him a blue parakeet and he wanted a yellow one. A gift certificate to the pet shop is a far better option.

***Remember:*** Holidays are the worst time to give a live animal to anyone. Holidays are traditionally busy times with lots of bustle and activity, and the poor parakeet may get lost in the shuffle. The holidays are a good time to buy bird books (such as this one!) and a gift certificate for the parakeet and the accessories that go with him.

# *To Breed or Not to Breed?*

If you have two or more parakeets, you may want to breed them. But breeding parakeets isn't a matter of sticking two birds together and then waiting for the babies to arrive. You'd be surprised at how much worry and parenting *you* actually have to do.

Before you even *consider* breeding your parakeets, consider the following:

- ✔ **Are you prepared for the extra expenses you will incur while breeding your parakeets?** Expenses include the cost of equipment, potential veterinary visits, formula and housing for the youngsters, among many others.

- ✔ **Are your birds in perfect health?** How do you know? When was the last time they had a regular checkup at your avian veterinarian? If you breed birds who aren't in perfect health, you run the risk of ending up with offspring who — you guessed it — aren't in perfect health.

- ✔ **Do you have a regular avian veterinarian who will take your calls at all hours when something goes wrong with the parents or the babies?** Raising baby birds isn't easy, and if you do so, you'll need access to an expert 24/7.

- ✔ **Are you able to handle the fact that you may lose one or more of your parakeets to breeding complications?** Watching a baby bird die isn't easy, but it's often a fact of life.

- ✔ **Will you care when your previously tame parakeets become nippy and territorial?** When your birds have babies, their focus is no longer on being your companion — their focus is on protecting their young.

✔ **Do you have the time and the know-how to hand-feed the young if the parents reject them?** Birds do sometimes reject their babies, and if that happens, you'll have to care for the young'uns constantly (see Figure 2-2).

✔ **Can you handle giving away or selling your precious babies?** Unless you have the room for a large flock of birds, you'll need to find a home for each of the babies — and not just *any* home, but a good home.

✔ **Are you prepared to keep all the babies if you can't find homes for them or they turn out handicapped in some way?** When you bring new babies into the world, you're responsible for caring for them. And if you can't find a home for all your babies, you'll have to keep them yourself.

These questions are only some of the things you'll have to consider when you embark on parakeet husbandry. Often, it's more trouble than it's worth. On the other hand, after you gain some experience, it can be a fun and rewarding hobby, especially if your goal is to breed English budgies for show purposes.

If you *don't* want your pair to breed, simply don't offer them anything nest-like, such as a dark, cozy place to sleep, like a box or a bird hut. They'll be fine sleeping on a perch. If they insist on breeding anyway and nesting on the bottom of the cage or in the seed dish, they may be getting too much light. Cut back their light to ten hours a day and cut out some of the protein that you're feeding them. This approach should calm their hormones a bit.

© Isabelle Francais

**Figure 2-2:** If your parakeet rejects her babies, hand-feeding is a must.

# Chapter 3

# Finding and Selecting a Parakeet

*F*inding the "perfect" parakeet may seem easy — just go to the pet shop and pick one out, right? Well, that's one way of doing it, but doing your homework may help in your final decision. If you've already gotten your parakeet by pointing into a cage and saying "Just give me one," you're not alone. In fact, I'll admit now that the last two parakeets I bought were from a pet shop, just little faces in the crowd. They're hard to resist, aren't they?

## Choosing a Parakeet: Exploring Your Options

You can find many "kinds" of parakeets — tamed, untamed, different colors, and previously owned parakeets, just to name a few. Which parakeet you should buy depends upon what you want or expect from the bird. In the following sections, I cover the main decisions you'll need to make before choosing the bird that's right for you.

### English budgie or American parakeet

The American parakeet and the English budgie are basically the same animal, except for size. The English budgie is more than twice the size of the American parakeet. It also has a shorter lifespan (about 7 years or so, as opposed to the American parakeet's 12 years or more), and its temperament can be a bit mellower than its smaller cousin.

If you want a hands-on companion, you'll find little difference in quality between the two birds, except that the English budgie may be a little easier to tame. Budgies are a little more difficult to breed, though, and can be at least four times more expensive than the American version.

## Fledgling or adult

A *fledgling* is a young bird that has just come out of the nest and is able to eat on its own. This is the best time to get a parakeet if you want it to be tame. Most baby parakeets are eating well on their own at 6 to 8 weeks of age and can be taken to a new home then. Some breeders may want to wait a little longer before they sell the babies, to make certain that they're strong and healthy.

An adult bird that has already been tamed makes a great companion as well. Parakeets reach young adulthood at 6 to 9 months of age. If you get an adult that has never been handled by humans before, you'll have to spend more time taming him.

If you want a really tame and sweet baby, try to find a breeder who will hand-feed a baby for you. The breeder will take the baby away from the parents while the bird is still reliant on them, and take over the parental duties. A bird who has been hand-fed as a baby will become very tame, because he'll be used to being handled.

So how do you know how old a bird is? You can tell the age of your new parakeet in three ways:

- ✔ **Leg band:** Most breeders put identification bands of the legs of their nestlings — the laws in many states require any birds sold to be banded. The band will have the breeder's ID engraved on it, as well as the state, the year hatched, and a number unique to your particular bird.

- ✔ **Barring on the head:** Baby parakeets have barring on the head (see Figure 3-1) and adults do not. The stripes disappear and are replaced by a solid color as the bird gets older.

- ✔ **The cere:** The *cere* is the bit of flesh just above the beak and is very blue in adult males and pink or brown in adult females. The cere is whitish/pinkish/bluish in babies, signifying that the parakeet is still young.

© Isabelle Francais

**Figure 3-1:** A young parakeet still has barring on the top of its head.

## Blue or green or . . .

Parakeets come in over 70 colors and more colors and patterns are being developed each year. Even so, you'll probably only find a few colors (for example, white, blue, violet, yellow, pied, and gray) in your local pet shop, and the bird's color has absolutely no effect on the quality of the bird. And no one color will make a better companion — simply choose the color you're most attracted to.

 The wild budgie is green, the base color from which all the other colors were developed. Those other colors (any color other than green) are called *mutations* and are a natural occurrence in nature that budgie breeders have capitalized on by breeding those mutated birds to one another until they produced others.

## Male or female

If you're buying your parakeet as a baby, you won't know its gender. No matter — just choose the one that you like. Males and females make equally good companions. Males tend to be more docile and females a little more feisty when they reach maturity, but this isn't always the case, especially if the bird is getting a lot of hands-on attention.

Males are better talkers than females, however, which is a consideration. Females can learn a few words and will learn to whistle, but males can learn hundreds of words and phrases. This doesn't mean that your male parakeet will definitely learn to talk — like everything else, this is based on the individual personality of the bird.

# Finding a Parakeet

After you've decided which traits you're looking for in a parakeet, you have to go out and find him. Fortunately, you have a variety of options — so if one place doesn't have what you're looking for, you can try another.

## Pet shops

Your local pet shop should have a cage full of parakeets, all ready to go home with you. Just today, I visited the pet shop on my corner to look at the birds — they must have had 60 parakeets, mostly green, blue, and yellow.

The concern with the *average* general pet shop is that the employees are busy with so many different animals and so many different dry-good products that they may not know a heck of a lot about birds (such as where the parakeets came from and how to recognize a sick bird when they see one). So before you buy a bird in a pet shop, you want to pay close attention to the store itself, as well as to the store's employees.

When you first walk into the pet store, ask yourself the following questions about the store:

- ✔ **Is the pet shop clean?** If not, get out of there right away.

- ✔ **Do the birds have clean water?** If the water looks like Mississippi mud, not only should you leave; you should tell the store manager before you do so.

- ✔ **Do the birds have food?** Again, tell the manager if they don't.

- ✔ **Do the parakeets have enough room?** Overcrowding is a stressful situation for birds — you're better off finding a store that doesn't cram its livestock. If the birds have hardly any perch space and they're scrambling all over each other, the cage probably doesn't offer enough room.

✔ **Do the birds look healthy?** If you see any parakeets sleeping on the floor of the cage, looking kind of puffy, that's a warning sign that the birds are sick. Leave these birds alone.

✔ **Does the staff know what a parakeet is?** If you ask for a parakeet and the salesperson starts to put a canary in a box for you, that's not a good sign.

✔ **Is the staff helpful and friendly?** Don't bother with a store that has hostile sales staff — they won't be helpful if you have a problem with your bird after you get him home.

If you answer "no" to any of these questions, move on and find another pet store — one where every answer is a "yes."

Whether you buy from a general pet shop or a birds-only store, you should ask some questions before about your potential parakeet before you consider taking him home:

✔ **Where do you get your parakeets?** If the employee doesn't know, reconsider buying from that store. If the employee is very nice and she says, "The owner breeds and hand-raises them himself. He's been a parakeet fancier for years," that's the best answer you can get.

✔ **Does this parakeet come with a health guarantee?** If the salesperson says, "What's that?" run fast and far away from there. (See the nearby sidebar on health guarantees.)

✔ **What is this parakeet eating?** "I dunno," is a terrible answer. "Seeds, what else would it eat?" is equally poor. If the answer is that all the birds are fed seeds/pellets plus fruits and vegetables and other fresh foods, you're likely to be happier with a bird from that store.

✔ **How old is this parakeet?** The store employees should be certain of the bird's age. *Remember:* For the fastest taming results, you'll want a young bird.

## Health guarantees

As with anything else, *buyer beware*. If you buy a bird without a health guarantee and your parakeet keels over, you're stuck with a dead parakeet and no recourse. Most good stores allow you a certain amount of time to take your bird for a checkup and will take the bird back if there's a problem. If you have no health guarantee, then you're buying the bird at your own risk.

## The swap meet

You can often find parakeets sold at your local swap meet or flea market, but be aware that if you buy a parakeet from a swap meet, you may not be able to find the person who sold it to you the very next week. Try to get a business card or a phone number when you purchase your bird so that you have someone to call if something goes wrong.

## The newspaper

Sometimes breeders advertise in the newspaper. The breeder may be a small-time breeder, with just a few pairs and some babies to sell. This may be a good choice because you may get to see where your bird came from and may even make a friend out of the seller, a person who can help you if you have trouble with your parakeet.

Meet in a safe, neutral place for the exchange. *Remember:* This is a stranger you've met from an ad the newspaper.

## Parakeet breeders

If you're very lucky, you'll find a parakeet *breeder,* someone who breeds for mutations and for showing. This person can even become a mentor to you, helping you become more knowledgeable in the hobby, if you decide to breed your own birds someday. You can also find a breeder through your local bird club. Most bird clubs also have shows or expos each year, which is a great place to meet bird fanatics.

When you arrive at the breeder's home, look for cleanliness and check to see if the birds are being treated humanely. Do they have enough space? Do they have fresh, clean water? Is the temperature too warm or too cold? If you feel comfortable with the conditions of the birds, then you should be comfortable buying one from this person.

Ask for a health guarantee and the right to return your parakeet should it not get a clean bill of health from your avian veterinarian.

## Bird shows

If you're lucky, you may find a bird show in your area, or if you're very lucky, a big English budgie show. Very often, breeders from around the country will bring their birds to show and to sell. A bird show is a great place to meet people and to see all kind of different colored parakeets. Your local bird club will probably hold a yearly show. Most bird clubs have Web sites — simply go to your favorite Internet search engine and type in "bird club society" plus the name of your town or the nearest large city, and you should come up with something.

 Walk around the show and talk to everyone. Take down some numbers and make some friends. These people are the ones who know the most about your parakeet and who can help and advise you with any situation you may encounter.

# Searching for a Healthy Parakeet

When you've decided on the color, age, gender, and type of parakeet you want, and you've decided where you're going to buy the bird, you have to go about choosing a healthy one. Choosing a healthy bird is actually easier than you may think.

 You may be tempted to buy a sleepy, sick looking bird. Of course, if you're a bird lover, how can you turn away from him? Do what feels right to you, but buying a sick bird is often a mistake. You risk infecting your other birds, you'll incur a huge veterinary bill, and the bird may not survive anyway.

 When you buy your parakeet, you should make a well-bird checkup appointment with your avian veterinarian, just to make sure the bird is as healthy as he looks.

You'll need to be on the lookout for several traits when you're shopping for a healthy parakeet:

- ✔ **Eyes:** A healthy parakeet's eyes are round, clear, and bright. You shouldn't see any crust or discharge from the eyes. The eyes should show seem alert — as if the bird is ready for action!

- ✔ **Nose and nares:** A parakeet's nostrils are called *nares* and they're located on the *cere*, which is the fleshy part just above the beak. The nares should be clean and without discharge. The cere should not be crusty or peeling.

- ✔ **Feathers:** The feathers of a healthy parakeet are shiny and tight, laying flat against the body (see Figure 3-2). A parakeet with excessively ruffled feathers may be ill. Feathers should cover the whole body — if you notice bald patches, the parakeet has a problem. The only acceptable reason for a parakeet to have patches of feathers missing is if his or her mate is pulling them out. They may also be suffering from having too small of a cage.

✔ **Feet:** A parakeet should have two feet (preferably, though some do fine with one) and the feet should be clean and free of debris. The parakeet should be able to perch easily on both feet. Sometimes a parakeet becomes crippled in the nest and can have splayed legs or other foot problems — but this is no reason to turn it away. A crippled parakeet still has its wings and will be able to get around if allowed full flight in a large cage (*full flight* means that the bird's wing feathers aren't clipped).

✔ **Vent:** The *vent* is on the bottom of the bird and is the place where waste is eliminated and where eggs are laid. The vent should be clean, and not crusted with feces or other material.

✔ **Attitude:** A healthy parakeet is active and chattery, always on the move. A parakeet who is sitting on the bottom of the cage, fluffed and sleepy, may be having a health problem. Try to choose a parakeet who is wandering around the cage socializing, eating, and bathing — this bird may be healthier than Mr. Sleepy in the corner of the cage, tying to get away from the others.

© Isabelle Francais

**Figure 3-2:** Healthy birds have clean, tight feathers and round shiny eyes.

# Chapter 4

# Home Tweet Home: Preparing for Your Parakeet

After you've chosen your perfect parakeet, you have to choose the perfect housing. Buying a cage and just sticking the new bird in it is like buying a house but not furnishing it. Many accessories come with a parakeet pad, and this chapter helps you choose the right ones.

## Your Parakeet's Home

Having Polly flying around the house 24 hours a day isn't safe or practical. Your parakeet needs a place to rest, eat, and play. Though birds aren't really meant to be caged (a wild bird would shudder at the thought), a cage is the most practical piece of equipment that you and your bird will own.

A cage should be used as your parakeet's home, not as its prison. Even if you buy Polly the nicest cage on the market and equip it with all kinds of goodies and toys, those things don't replace the exercise and stimulation that your parakeet will get from being out of her cage every day.

### Size is everything

The old saying "bigger is better" refers to more than bird cages, but the saying works for them, too. When you're looking for a cage for your parakeet, look for the largest cage that the space in your home and your budget will allow.

If the salesperson at the pet shop tells you that a cage is good for a few parakeets, it's probably good for one or two. That's the one to buy.

When you go to the pet store, you'll find some cages labeled as parakeet cages, and you may be tempted to trust the label. These are usually small, pastel-colored cages geared toward being kept in a child's room. This kind of cage is an unacceptable home for your parakeet *unless* she's out of her cage and interacting with you for most of the day. In any other case, you should buy a much larger cage.

A cage that's labeled as a "flight cage" isn't really a flight cage — after all, how much flying can a bird do in 2 feet of space? However, this cage may be a better choice than the tiny pastel cages.

Even though a cage is large, it may not be acceptable for a parakeet. Make certain that the bars of the cage are not wide enough for your parakeet to stick her head through. If she sticks her head through the bars in the cage, she could be injured, or even die, as she struggles to get free.

## Looking at shape

Square or rectangular cages are far better than round ones. Your parakeet will like a corner to bunch himself into when he's scared or sleepy, and a round cage doesn't offer that comfort. Square or rectangular cages also offer more cage space for the same basic cage size.

## Considering cage materials

Most typical cages are made of metal and plastic, and some are coated to add a color or a texture. Metal cages are preferable to wooden cages, which are often sold to finch owners. Although wooden cages are attractive, your parakeet will certainly begin to destroy it in no time.

Be careful that the coating on the outside is nontoxic and won't harm your birds. If you notice that your parakeet is picking away at the coating, *remove him from the cage immediately* and get a new cage that doesn't have a coating on the bars. Ingestion of this coating can be deadly.

Cages made entirely or partially of acrylic eliminate a lot of mess. These cages are much more expensive than the standard metal cages, but they're attractive, safe, and can save you some time cleaning. Some even come with mechanical ventilation that cleans the air inside the cage — a nice feature for those who suffer from allergies. The downside is that acrylic cages lack bars, and the bars allow for climbing, which is a favorite pastime of a caged parakeet.

## Keeping safety in mind

You'd hope that all bird cages were safe, but unfortunately, that's not the case. When you're in the market for a cage for your parakeet, you want to make sure that you choose one that will keep your bird safe and healthy.

Some decorative cages have scrollwork that can catch a toe and cause bleeding, which can be dangerous and painful for a little bird such as a parakeet. Look for simplicity in a cage.

Many cages have guillotine-style doors that can snap down onto a little feathered head and break a neck. These doors open from the bottom and are quite weighty. You're better off finding a cage with doors that open from the side, like the door to a house, or that open from the top and pull down. If you have a cage with the guillotine-style doors, invest in inexpensive spring clips from the hardware store. These clips will prevent a potential escape artist from having his little feathered neck clamped in a heavy door.

Your cage must have a grating on the bottom to keep the bird away from her own mess. Line the tray beneath the grating with good old-fashioned newspaper, which has a disinfecting effect from the ink and makes it easy to see the droppings (you want to check your bird's dropping to see if she's ill). Several types of bird litter are on the market, and these are fine to use, too, but people tend to clean the cage less when they use litter because seeing the mess is more difficult. *Remember:* If you use bird litter, you should still clean the cage at least every other day, if not daily.

Using litter poses other dangers as well. They can become moist, allowing fungus and bacteria to grow, which can be deadly to your bird. Also, if the bedding is within reach of the bird, he can ingest it and may become ill, even die. In addition, never, ever use cedar shavings near any bird — these shavings may smell nice, but the fumes they emit can cause respiratory distress.

## Deciding where to put your bird's cage

Your parakeet will be most comfortable placed close to a wall or in a corner, so that only two of the four sides of the cage are facing the great wide open. The wall(s) will afford your parakeet the feeling of safety. A cage that's hung from a chain or placed out in the open may cause your parakeet to become nervous and frightened.

Your parakeet's cage is best placed in an area that is going to get *some* traffic — but not too much traffic. *Remember:* You're better off giving him too much attention than not enough.

The cage must be out of drafts and in a consistent temperature zone. If the room has wide temperature swings, you may want to consider a different spot. The bird's room should be dark and quiet for a good part of the night and sunny and bright (with artificial lights, if necessary) for most of the day.

There are some places where you should *never* place your parakeet's cage:

- ✔ **A child's bedroom:** Your parakeet won't get a lot of attention in a child's room and will be alone most of the day while your child is at school.

- ✔ **The floor:** A high spot will make your parakeet feel secure and a low spot will make him feel very uneasy, especially if you have other pets.

- ✔ **The bathroom:** This room is prone to wild temperature ranges that aren't good for your parakeet.

- ✔ **The kitchen:** Potential fumes and temperature swings will make your parakeet uncomfortable or ill — and they may even kill her. Many products in the kitchen are not safe for your bird.

- ✔ **Directly in front of a window:** There may be predators outside that will disturb and frighten your bird. Even cars going by can seem dangerous to a little parakeet.

# Accessorizing Your Parakeet's Abode

Cage accessories aren't optional — they're essential to your parakeet's health and happiness. You may invest in a bunch of accessories in the beginning and discover that you and your parakeet need many more items to keep both of you happy.

## *Perches, please!*

Additional perches are the first thing you'll want to think about buying for your parakeet's cage. Your bird spends all his time on his feet (if your parakeet is lying at the bottom of the cage, feet up, you may want to check to see if he's still breathing!). Because your parakeet uses his feet so much, you want him to be able to stand on perches with as many widths, materials, and textures as possible. Fortunately, many different kinds of perches are available to choose from, and they're readily available at your local pet shop.

 If your bird only has one type and size of perch to stand on, he can develop serious foot problems. Think of good perches as orthopedic shoes that can make all the difference between your bird staying happy and healthy and needing a visit to the veterinarian.

### *Wooden perches*

Wooden perches come in a variety of shapes, sizes, and types of wood. Regular pine perches are popular and are fun for your parakeet to chew. Manzanita perches are harder and last longer; they come in twisty shapes that look more natural than the usual wooden dowels. Cholla wood is also regularly used as perch material and has a natural texture that's good for the feet.

 You can use perches from your trees outside (see Figure 4-1), but you must be absolutely certain that the type of tree is nontoxic and that it was never sprayed with insecticide.

 Wooden perches need to be cleaned often. Wood is porous and can harbor bad bacteria. Scrub the perches weekly and then soak them in a 10 percent bleach solution once a month. Remember to rinse the perches thoroughly and allow them to dry completely before putting them back into the cage.

### *Plastic perches*

Plastic perches are popular because they're easy to clean and snap on and off the cage bars easily. These are a fine addition to your array of perches, but they shouldn't be the only kind of perch your bird has. Plastic is probably not as nice to stand on as wood or rope.

### *Rope perches*

Rope perches are made from cotton fibers, sisal, or a hemp-like material. These perches are terrific additions to your parakeet's cage. They come in a variety of diameters and can be twisted into all kinds of shapes to fit into your bird's cage.

© Isabelle Francais

**Figure 4-1:** Parakeets enjoy wooden perches of varying diameters.

If you use rope perches, be careful to trim all loose strands that may arise from your parakeet's chewing behavior. These loose stands can wind around a toe or foot and cause injury. Rope perches should be replaced often, especially if they frequently become damp.

### Concrete perches

Concrete perches are available in all sorts of colors and diameters and will often become a bird's favorite perch. This rough perch acts as a nail and beak trimmer. Every parakeet should have at least one of these perches along with the others. Many birds choose to sleep on the concrete perch at night.

Concrete perches are often used as a "napkin" on which your parakeet will wipe his beak after eating a particularly messy meal. This activity is great for the beak but not so great for the perch. Clean the perch often in warm soapy water and be sure to rinse it carefully before placing it back in the cage.

Many people are fans of sandpaper sheathes that slip over existing perches. These are actually not great for your parakeet's feet because the sheathes can become soiled easily and can harbor bacteria.

## Cups and bowls

The cage you purchased probably came with a couple of cups for seed and water, which is a good start, but you'll need a few more cups to complete your set.

You'll need other types of cups for the various food items you'll be feeding your parakeet. You may want to invest in *mess-free cups* as well — mess-free cups have little hoods on them that keep most of the seed in the cup, not on the floor. These can be real time-savers. However, don't use the hooded cups for water — your bird may want to take a bath, crawl inside, and not be able to get back out.

The cups that probably came with your cage are plastic, which is not the finest material for a bird cup. Plastic can become scratched and harbor bacteria in the grooves of the scratches, no matter how well you clean.

Stainless steel is a great material for bird cups. It's durable, easy to clean, and may even outlast your bird. Ceramic cups are also a good choice. Both of these types of cups can be found with holders that keep them secure in the cage to avoid seed dumping.

To keep your parakeet's cage clean and to save your valuable time, consider keeping two sets of dishes. This means that you'll have six dishes — two for seeds/pellets, two for water, and two for fresh foods. Each day, you'll remove the dirty dishes and replace them with the clean ones, allowing you to then disinfect the other dishes for tomorrow.

## Cage covers

Some parakeets really like their cages to be covered at night, and others may want to be covered only halfway or on three sides. Covering the cage offers a degree of security and protection. Your bird won't be disturbed from sleep by light in the house or a cat slinking around in the middle of the night. The cover protects from drafts as well, and the darkness in the cage may allow you more sleeping time if your bird generally likes to get up with the sun and you don't. Using a cover is like tucking your birds in at night.

Some parakeets will become frightened if their cage is covered all the way. Listen for thrashing and commotion at night. If you sense that your birds are disturbed by the cover, only cover the cage partially so that your parakeet can look out and see what's making that noise at night (probably someone making a midnight snack!).

A fitted cage cover will fit snugly around the cage and allow for the maximum protection from light and drafts. It's also good for covering the cage in the daytime when your bird may need a nap or some quiet time. Don't cover your bird for more than an hour a day, and never use the cover as a muting devise for a lengthy period of time. A parakeet's chatter and singing is part of his charm.

## Mineral and beak blocks

A *mineral block* and a *beak block* are essentially the same thing — a lump of minerals shaped into a block or, nowadays, into a fun fruit or vegetable shape. Your parakeet will appreciate this treat and it will help to keep his beak trim. The block also adds some calcium to his diet.

## Swings

Parakeets love swings — there's not doubt about it. Don't scrimp in the swing department. Your parakeet will love one with toys and do-dads on it — the more the better.

## Baths

Bathing is essential for your parakeet — it's good for your parakeet's skin and is a natural behavior, even if it's a bit messy in the cage.

Preventing your bird from bathing is a terrible idea — and so is forcing your bird to bathe. Your bird knows when it's time for a bath and he'll do it when he feels like it.

Most birds bathe in their water dish, which will require you to clean it more often. Provide your parakeet with a separate bath (larger than the watering dish) that he may prefer.

The standard little bathtub with a mirror in the bottom is particularly popular with parakeets. They can bathe and admire themselves at the same time! You can also buy the kind of bath that hangs outside the cage from one of the doors — a nice option because it keeps the water contained.

## You light up my life

If you're like me and live in a part of the country that gets cold and dark for a good portion of the year, you'll want to invest in bird lamps. You can get special bulbs that have a wide spectrum of light that mimic the sun's rays — well, not exactly, but they're better than your standard light bulb.

Buy a standard, cheap spot lamp from the hardware store and clip it a few feet away from your parakeet's cage, shining the bird light directly at the birds. Some of these bulbs offer a bit of heat too, which is great in the wintertime, though you don't want to put the light so close that it heats the birds too much.

If you can't find bird-specific bulbs, buy bulbs made for reptiles — they're basically the same thing.

# Recognizing the Importance of Toys

Toys are vital to the health and well-being of a single parakeet. A pair can get along fairly well without them, but why should they have to? Toys will make up the majority of your parakeet's "job." Wild parakeets work all day at finding food and water and at staying safe. Your parakeet doesn't get nearly this much exercise, though he does require it.

Giving your parakeet lots of fun toys will allow him to achieve a level of activity that he wouldn't get if he didn't have the toys. Toys are for chewing and flinging, for preening and for arguing with. A beloved toy can offer a lonely parakeet a sense of comfort and a sense of home.

## Typical toys for parakeets

The typical parakeet toy is small, may be plastic or wooden, and often contains a bell. Parakeets love shiny, interactive toys that they can fling around or lavish with affection. You may have noticed that some toys for parakeets are directed toward alleviating loneliness (such as mirror toys, floss and preening toys, or toys shaped like another life-sized parakeet).

Parakeets are destructive, but they aren't very powerful, which is why there are so many plastic toys on the market geared toward them. These products are fine, but you may want to consider a mixture of wooden, rope, and plastic toys — this will give your parakeet a variety to choose from.

Mirror toys are popular for the single parakeet. Though this is a fun and interactive toy, your parakeet may become so enamored with his reflection that he forgets about you and about his training. He may sit staring into his reflection all day, marveling at what a beautiful and charming mate he has managed to woo, a regular

Narcissus. If you notice that Polly is becoming way to affectionate with his mirror, you may want to remove it temporarily, until his affections return to you.

## Jungle gyms: Not just for gymnasts

No parakeet's furniture is complete without a play gym. A play gym usually consists of a platform affixed with perches, ladders (see Figure 4-2), and toys. This gives your bird ample opportunity to play and get some much-needed activity.

Many of these gyms come with food cups — playtime may be a good occasion to entice your parakeet to try new foods. A play gym is also a great training tool because you can place him on the steady perch and work with him there, instead of trying to work with him close to his cage, where he may seek refuge.

I have multiple play gyms all over my house, especially in places where I've noticed that my birds were becoming destructive, like on top of my cable box. I simply set a play gym on top of it and the birds can no longer get to those tasty buttons — though they can still sit there and look out the window.

© Isabelle Francais

**Figure 4-2:** Parakeets love to climb around on ladders like this one.

## *Watch out!: Avoiding unsafe toys*

Not all toys are safe for your parakeet. He has a very tiny head that can get caught in a plastic or metal ring, or he can catch his toes in little places, such as the slots in a jingle bell. Check all your new toys carefully before placing them in your parakeet's cage.

 Old toys with sharp corners or fraying rope can be dangerous as well. File sharp corners with a nail file and trim any loose strings that could potentially get wrapped around a neck or a foot.

# *Keeping Messes at Bay*

Even if you have only one parakeet, it may seem to you that the mess in your home has doubled. You can't keep your parakeet from making messes, but you can contain the mess he makes. You can also take advantage of some easy ways to save time cleaning up — without having to hire a butler or a maid (though the butler or maid would be nice, huh?).

The most surefire way of keeping your floor clean is to not allow the seed to fall there in the first place. Cage bloomers and seed guards, available at your local pet shop, can be a huge help. Both products fit snugly around the cage bottom and create a barrier so that most of the seed stays in the cage tray.

 If your birds are like mine and are determined to make a mess regardless of the bloomer, you may have to take more-drastic measures. I went to my local fabric shop and purchased a few yards of clear plastic, like the kind someone may use for a tablecloth. It's nontoxic and easy to handle. I covered three of the four sides on all of my cages with this material, and it stopped the mess by 90 percent. I left the top and the front of the cage uncovered but placed a flap of the plastic in front, where the food and water dishes are. It works very well.

By far, the handiest item in your cleaning kit is the handheld vacuum. This little machine is your remedy to utter disarray. I probably use mine three or four times a day — if I didn't, my floor would be covered (my birds are out most of the day, flinging seed and paper around).

 Many household cleansers are deadly to your bird, so you don't want to use them in or around your bird's cage. Instead, you can use natural disinfectants such as vinegar for cleaning the cage and baking soda for scrubbing. If you have a real mess, you can use a

10 percent bleach solution for soaking (1 cup bleach per 10 cups water), but always make sure to rinse very carefully before returning anything soaked in bleach to your bird.

You can buy special bird-safe cleaners at the pet shop, which work rather well and often smell pretty good. Nothing makes up for good old elbow grease and safe household cleansers like vinegar or baking soda — don't mix vinegar and baking soda, though, or you'll get an interesting chemical reaction that may force you to do more cleaning!

Clean the paper in the bottom of the cage every day or every other day. Scrape off any dried droppings once a week, and soak the entire cage in soapy water or a 10 percent bleach solution about every ten days. If you're a neatnik and want to clean more than this, feel free!

# Parakeet-Proofing Your Home

If you're going to allow your parakeet time out of the cage, even if you think that you're going to supervise him all the time, you have to parakeet-proof your home. Even if you have a pair that isn't going to leave the cage, the average home has items that can be harmful, even deadly, to a little parakeet. In the following sections, I cover tips to keep your home safe for your new companion.

## Make sure all windows are screened

Parakeets are excellent flyers, and even a partially clipped parakeet will be able to soar away. Many people lose their parakeets through an open window or door, especially if more than one person lives in the household. One person may open a window and another person may let the bird out of the cage, neither knowing what the other has done.

Either keep your parakeet's wings clipped or build a flight cage or aviary where your birds can fly safely without the danger of flying away. Be sure that your aviary is predator-safe and has shelter from the elements.

## Keep your windows and mirrors a little dirty

Your parakeet will think that a window or mirror is actually more space, and she may soar right into it. Keeping your windows and your mirrors dirty is a great way to help avoid this kind of heartbreaking accident.

If you're a four-star housekeeper, place stickers on your windows and mirrors, because the bird may mistake the glass for open space and fly right into it.

## Get rid of (or at least turn off) the ceiling fan

Ceiling fans are an absolute no-no when it comes to your parakeet. Your parakeet may fly up there while it's on and get injured, or worse. One whoosh of a whirling blade and he's history. Keep ceiling fans off when your parakeet is out of the cage.

## Keep your house free of artificial scents

Parakeets have an extremely delicate respiratory system. Scents that may not bother you — like those from a scented candle or an air freshener — can kill a parakeet.

## Avoid all products with nonstick coatings

When it's heated, the nonstick coating used on many types of cookware and other products emits a fume that has been proven to kill birds, so be sure never to use such products as long as you're a bird owner.

Even if your parakeet is in another part of the house from where you're cooking, the fumes still travel — they've even been known to kill birds through walls in apartment buildings.

Products that use nonstick coating (and that should be avoided at all costs) include the following:

- Anything that says it is "nonstick"
- Bread machines
- Broiler pans
- Coffeemakers
- Cooking utensils (with nonstick coating)
- Crock pots
- Curling irons
- Deep fryers
- Drip pans for burners
- Electric skillets
- Griddles

- ✔ Hairdryers with nonstick coils
- ✔ Heat lamps
- ✔ Ironing-board covers
- ✔ Irons
- ✔ Lollipop molds
- ✔ Ovens with nonstick coating (which burns off after the first use or when being self-cleaned)
- ✔ Pizza pans
- ✔ Popcorn poppers
- ✔ Portable heaters
- ✔ Roasters
- ✔ Rolling pins (the nonstick variety)
- ✔ Stockpots
- ✔ Stovetop burners
- ✔ Waffle makers
- ✔ Woks

I know that this list is long, and it may seem that you have to change your whole life for your parakeet. Some people do use some of these items successfully if their homes are very well ventilated and the nonstick item is being used far away from the parakeet. In any case, the most crucial of these is the cookware — most bird keepers don't use it, and I recommend you don't either.

## Tuck away all electrical cords

Electrical cords may look like fun rope toys — with deadly consequences. Even if fraying electrical cords are not your bird's idea of fun, he can certainly land on them and knock over a lamp or other appliance, possibly injuring himself and others. Keep all cords neatly tucked away behind furniture.

## Check your home for lead and other metals

Lead is deadly for humans and it's just as deadly for parakeets. That beautiful stained-glass frame hanging near the birdcage contains lead, as does peeling and chipping paint and many fishing weights.

Some people build their own cages, which is a great way to get the size and shape of cage that you want, but most caging wire is galvanized, meaning that it has a coating of zinc on it, a metal that is highly toxic to birds. Scrub any new caging material before putting your birds inside their new home.

## Put all medications away, out of reach of your parakeet

Birds are inquisitive and may get into a package of medicine that you thought was packed tight. These little nibblers can break into a thin cardboard box and break the foil over your allergy or cold and flu pills, so don't make the mistake of thinking that a box of pills is safe. Try to keep all your medicines in childproof plastic bottles.

## Make sure your parakeet doesn't have access to standing water

Fish tanks, toilet bowls, and even Fido's water dish all pose a drowning threat to a parakeet. Parakeets can even drown in a glass of water while trying to take a drink.

## Remove all toxic houseplants from your parakeet's reach

Some houseplants are perfectly safe for nibbling and others are extremely deadly. If you don't know whether a plant is toxic, find out from your local library — or be safe and don't let your bird near it at all.

Your parakeet may like to chew on tree cuttings from the outdoors, but be absolutely sure that the branches you give him have not been sprayed with *any* kind of pesticides or fertilizers — these chemicals can be instantly deadly to your parakeet.

## Make sure that predators can't reach your parakeet

In all likelihood, your other pets (including dogs, cats, ferrets, and snakes) are keenly interested in your parakeet — and *not* just to make friends.

If you keep your parakeet outdoors, even part of the time, be aware that birds of prey such as hawks, owls, raccoons, rats, and opossums are extremely good at pulling a little bird right through the cage bars.

# A Happy Homecoming

Chances are that you'll have to travel with your parakeet at some point in his life — the first trip will be from the pet shop or breeder to your house. A pet store will send you home with the parakeet in a little cardboard box made for the temporary transport of small animals, but I recommend buying a real carrier from the get-go.

Use only a bird-specific carrier, one that's airline approved. If you start with a cheaper, plastic carrier, you're just going to have to buy the nicer one at some point anyway, so you may as well make the investment in the beginning. Most airline-approved carriers are made from a light plastic and have a grated opening on the front or the top. If you ever need to fly with your bird, you can simply put the carrier under your seat.

Small, thick plastic crocks for seed are good to use inside the carrier, as opposed to a heavier ceramic dish, which can move quickly and trap or injure your parakeet. Don't use a water dish during traveling, but another plastic crock into which you put fruits and vegetables, which will give your bird the moisture that he needs during his trip. If the trip is very long, you can give him a dish of water for a few minutes every few hours. Water in the carrier is likely to spill and cause your parakeet discomfort.

I had a potter make me a special ceramic dish for my birds' travels — it's round and has a lip that reaches over the top of the dish. Water can slosh around but it can't spill, and the bird can have a drink if he wants one.

You won't need to use perches inside the carrier, which can cause injury to a parakeet that is trying hard to hang on to it. Your parakeet will be fine on the bottom of the carrier.

If you're traveling by car, make sure that the sun isn't shining directly on the carrier — parakeets can be overcome by heat very quickly. If the weather is chilly, bring a towel with you and cover the carrier with it.

# Chapter 5

# Polly Want a Cracker?
# Caring for Your Parakeet

. . . . . . . . . . . . . . . . . . . . . . . . . . . . . . . . . . . . . . .

## In This Chapter

▶ Feeding your parakeet properly

▶ Understanding why and how to clip your parakeet's wing feathers

▶ Getting some exercise (for your bird, that is)

. . . . . . . . . . . . . . . . . . . . . . . . . . . . . . . . . . . . . . .

*P*arakeets are prone to all kinds of nutritional disorders, many of which can be deadly. They are notorious fatties, gorging on seed to the exclusion of just about everything else if you let them. Obesity is a huge (pardon the pun) health issue for parakeets, so it's important to ensure that your bird gets the proper nutrition he needs to live out his lifespan in good health. Exercise and grooming are important parts of your parakeet's care as well. This chapter helps you care for and nourish your parakeet, inside and out.

## *Water, Water Everywhere . . .*

In the wild, parakeets base their daily activities on finding water, flying for many miles each day to drink. The wild parakeet's breeding season revolves around rain, and the number of chicks successfully hatched is dependant on how much water is available to the parents. (You can tell this story to your parakeet the next time he gives you attitude.)

 Try not to use water straight from the tap as your bird's drinking water. Tap water contains chlorine, metals, and other toxins, which are bad for your parakeet. Bottled drinking water or filtered water is a much better option.

Do not let your parakeet's water become filthy. Change your bird's water no less than twice a day. Dirty water can harbor bacteria that are potentially harmful for your bird. Your parakeet's water dishes should be clean enough for *you* to drink out of them.

An easy way to ensure that your bird's water remains fresh is to have two sets of water dishes — one for the morning water and one for the evening water. Soak water dishes in a 10 percent bleach solution once a week to sterilize them. Rinse the water dishes thoroughly before returning them to your parakeet's cage.

If you have a tube-style waterer, or a product called a "two-week waterer," you still must change the water daily. If you don't, your parakeet could get sick. Just because the package says "two-week waterer" doesn't mean that you don't have to change the water for two weeks!

# Can I Get Some Food around Here?: Knowing What Your Parakeet Should (and Shouldn't) Eat

Companion parakeets do well on a seed-*based* diet, but they can't live on seeds alone. Seed is full of carbs and fat, and only a lifestyle high in exercise (like the kind of lifestyle wild parakeets have) can burn off all those calories. An all-seed diet will cause your parakeet to develop serious health issues and will shorten its already short life by *years*.

In the following sections, I let you know what kinds of foods your parakeet needs and wants, what foods you should *never* feed your parakeet, and how to supplement your parakeet's diet.

## What to feed your parakeet

Each species of bird has its own dietary requirements, and the parakeet is no exception. In the following sections, I cover the many kinds of foods you can and should feed your parakeet.

No matter what kind of food you feed your parakeet, always offer as much as the bird will eat. You don't have to ration your bird's feed. The only time you may want to ration is with seeds, and in this case you will be replacing the seeds with other foods, so your parakeet should never go hungry. Parakeets have a very fast metabolism, and even one day without food can cause problems — more than that can cause death.

## Seeds

Because parakeets are seed-eaters in the wild, your pet parakeet will relish seed. Seeds fill your parakeet's stomach, and he's used to it.

I recommend that you *do* offer seed in small amounts, but certainly not as the bird's entire diet. Your veterinarian may suggest that you don't feed seed at all — and that choice is up to you. If you convert your bird to another type of diet — pellets, for example — then there is no reason to offer seeds beyond the fact that your bird likes them.

Seeds are not a *bad* food — they're just often misused. Many veterinarians suggest that people take their birds off of seeds because they feel that owners may not be responsible enough to provide a diverse and healthful diet for their birds. (Seeds add a lot of carbohydrates and fat to your bird's diet, things that a wild parakeet needs far more than your companion bird does.)

Some of the seed mixes in the pet shop are brightly colored and claim to be "fortified" with vitamins. The fact is that the vitamins are in the coloring that the manufacturer coats on the *outside* of the seed, while the inside of the seed, the only part that your parakeet actually eats, remains the same. Save your money and buy the regular seed, and spend the money on healthy fruits and vegetables for your bird instead.

Seeds that have been sprouted are much higher in nutrition than dry seeds and make a nutritious treat. You can find already sprouted beans at the supermarket

## Pellets

Pellets emerged on the bird scene a number of years ago and have quickly become a trend in feeding birds. Pellets are a combination of ingredients that the manufacturer shapes into bits that resemble seeds and other shapes that birds find interesting.

As with seeds, pellets are not *bad,* but they are not the only food you should feed your parakeet. Variety is essential. Pellets are an okay base diet, but feeding them does not mean that you should exclude other foods, such as fruits and vegetables, table foods, and some seeds.

Check the label on the pellets, and try to buy only all-natural, preservative-free, organic pellets.

### Fruits and vegetables

Vegetables and fruits are a great way to get important vitamins and minerals into your parakeet, and they make a fun addition to the diet as well. Try to feed your parakeet at least five fresh vegetables or fruits a day. Eventually, you'll get to know what your parakeet's favorites are and you can keep them on hand.

How you serve fruits and veggies depends on the type of fruit or veggie. For example, your parakeet will like broccoli florets, apple wedges, shredded cabbage, whole or shredded greens (leaves), peas out of the pod, green beans chopped, and carrots (whole, chopped, shredded, or cooked). Experiment with how you serve fruits and veggies — if your parakeet doesn't eat it one way, she may be temped to try it another way. Also, when serving fruit, make sure to remove any seeds or pits — these can be toxic.

Here's a list of vegetables that are good for your parakeet:

- beans (cooked)
- broccoli
- cabbage
- carrots
- cauliflower
- cucumbers
- endive
- green beans
- greens (all varieties)
- hot peppers
- kale
- peas
- potato (cooked)
- soy beans
- spinach
- watercress
- yams
- zucchini

Here's a list of fruits that are good for your parakeet:

- apples
- bananas
- berries (all varieties)
- cantaloupes
- figs
- grapes (with skin)
- honeydew
- kiwis
- mangoes
- oranges
- peaches
- pears
- pineapples
- plums
- tangerines

Deep green or orange produce have the most nutrients, especially vitamin A, which your parakeet needs to be healthy. Vitamin A–deficient birds are prone to respiratory problems and skin and liver problems.

Wash all fruit and vegetables thoroughly before serving. Your parakeet can be affected by even the tiniest traces of pesticides. If you can, offer organic produce so you have one less thing to worry about.

Fruits and vegetables sour quickly in warm weather, so remove them a few hours after you offer them. You can leave these foods in the cage longer in cooler weather, but if you put them out in the morning, make sure to remove them in the evening.

### Snacks

A great many bird snacks are on the market, many of them seed-based. Your parakeet will relish a snack like this, but realize that he may prefer it to healthier foods (just as you may prefer chocolate to cauliflower). Only offer a seed-based treat to your parakeet once a month or so.

Millet spray is another treat that your parakeet will *love.* The millet spray looks like a little tree branch with hundreds of seeds attached to it (see Figure 5-1). Again, you shouldn't let your bird gorge on it. Offer millet spray once or twice a week.

**Figure 5-1:** Parakeets love millet spray as a treat.

# Converting to pellets

If you decide to convert your parakeet from a seed-based diet to a pellet-based diet, you must first get the go-ahead from your avian veterinarian. Conversion is stressful, and your parakeet must be in prime condition before you make the switch. Never try to convert breeding birds or sick birds, and *never* make your parakeet switch cold turkey — this can lead to starvation and death.

After your veterinarian approves the switch, mix the pellets with the seed at a 50:50 ratio so that your parakeet gets used to seeing the pellets. Each week, gradually reduce the ratio of seeds to pellets, until you're only feeding pellets by the fifth week. Keep offering lots of other foods at this time as well, especially healthy fruits and vegetables.

You want to make sure that your parakeet is actually *eating* the pellets. Parakeets can starve themselves to death — and their health can be severely affected by not eating for even a day and a half.

Younger parakeets have an easier time converting than older parakeets, so start early. Some pet stores or breeders are already feeding pellets, so be sure to ask about the bird's diet before you bring him home.

## Table foods

Healthy table foods are a wonderful addition to your parakeet's diet. With a few exceptions, your bird can eat anything that you eat. Unlike dogs and cats, which can become ill from table foods, your parakeet may actually become healthier if you share your meals with him. And don't worry about spices — birds can eat the hottest of peppers and never flinch.

Eggs are also a great addition to your bird's diet, in any style. One great way to serve eggs is to boil them for about 30 minutes, cool them, and then crush them, shell and all. **Remember:** Make sure to boil the eggs well because those eggs came from a chicken that could potentially pass on a disease to your parakeet.

Your bird may enjoy some breakfast cereal, especially Cheerios, because he can hold the little *O*s in his beak and tote them around the cage. In the cold months, offer hot cereal, prepared and then cooled to just above room temperature.

"Birds eating birds" sounds like a sleazy talk-show topic, but in this case I'm referring to feeding your parakeet chicken and turkey meat. Believe it or not, a bit of these foods on occasion is very healthy, adding some protein to your parakeet's diet.

Whole-wheat and nutty-grain bread is a great snack every other day. It's especially good if you're breeding your parakeets because it's soft and easy to feed to the babies. Whole-wheat crackers are good, too, but be sure that they're not salty — salt-free crackers are best. Even low-sodium crackers may contain too much salt for your parakeets.

### Cooked foods

Several manufacturers have come out with a cooked food product for birds that you prepare once or twice a week and serve warm. Parakeets, as well as other birds, absolutely love this kind of food.

You'd do well to make these cooked diets the bird's base diet and offer fewer seeds and pellets.

## What not to feed your parakeet

Though *you* may eat a Twinkie or two while watching television, that doesn't mean your bird can share in the treat. *Never* indulge your bird with junk food of any kind. Salty, fatty, and sugary foods are terrible for your parakeet — they can even be deadly.

Birds can actually die from foods that we humans eat regularly. Here is a list of the *nevers* and why you shouldn't feed them:

- **Alcohol:** Put your bird on the wagon and don't ever share your margarita with him! Alcohol is toxic to birds and can cause death.

- **Avocado:** This tasty plant harbors an ingredient near the skin of its pit that is toxic to birds. Don't take the chance.

- **Caffeine:** Never give your bird sips of soda, tea, or coffee. Caffeine is toxic to birds.

- **Chocolate:** Birds metabolize chocolate differently from humans, and the result is toxic.

- **Onions (raw):** Cooked onions in something you're eating and want to share will probably be fine, but never feed your parakeet raw onions. (If you want to be safe, just avoid onions altogether.)

- **Pits and fruit seeds:** Remove all seeds and pits from fruits before you serve them to your parakeet. Some of these seeds are toxic.

- **Rhubarb:** This delicious vegetable can be toxic to your bird.

# *Nutritional supplements:*
# *When food isn't enough*

Like humans, parakeets can often benefit from dietary supplements. In the following sections, I cover some ways in which you may want to supplement your parakeet's diet.

Do not supplement before you speak to your avian veterinarian.

### *Vitamin A*

Parrot-type birds, such as your parakeet, need more vitamin A in their diet than humans do. Talk to your veterinarian about your parakeet's diet and the possibility of adding an emulsified vitamin A supplement to the water. Your avian veterinarian may opt for a better diet for your parakeet rather than a supplement.

Vitamin A is toxic at high levels. Before you consider offering a supplement, try to get your parakeet to eat fruits and vegetables that are rich in vitamin A, such as carrots, sweet potatoes, kale, spinach, butternut squash, mangoes, red peppers, and turnip greens.

Vitamins in any form tend to turn a parakeet's water into a bacteria soup. If you do decide to add vitamins to your parakeet's water, be sure that you change the water twice a day.

Many bird keepers add one or two drops of apple cider vinegar to their bird's water daily. The vinegar is said to ward off bacteria, and is even healthful for your bird. Be careful not to add too much, or the water will be too stinky to drink. Purchase organic vinegar if you can.

### *Oil supplements*

A few oil-based supplements on the market are healthful for your bird. These supplements keep the skin healthy and the feathers shiny. These oils are not going to hurt your bird, and they may even help — but they aren't particularly necessary if your bird is eating the way he should be. Talk to your veterinarian about the use of an oil supplement.

### *Powdered additives*

Because seeds lack many nutrients, a few companies produce a powered additive that you sprinkle onto the seed. The problem with them is that the powder often sifts through the seed and is not ingested by your bird. When used in conjunction with the oil-based supplement (see the preceding section), the powder will stick, making the seed a nutrient-rich food.

## Kiss my grits!

A common myth is that all birds need grit in their diet. Parakeets absolutely do *not* need it. Because parakeets *hull* their seeds (remove the outer shell from the seed and eat only the seed itself), the bird has no need for any kind of sand in the *gizzard* (the bird's "second stomach" that grinds the food). In fact, the presence of grit in the cage may incite the bird to gorge on it, stuffing up his digestive system with stones that won't come out, which can lead to health problems and death. The bottom line: Do not offer grit to your parakeet.

### Cuttlebones and mineral blocks

Cuttlebone is a good source of natural calcium. It actually comes from inside the cuttlefish, a type of squid. Hang the cuttlebone on the side of the cage near a perch, and watch your bird pick at it and play with it.

Some people are concerned with the source of the cuttlebone, fearing that the squid may be harvested in polluted waters. If you want, you can opt instead for a mineral block, which is a good source of calcium (many contain other minerals as well). You can use a mineral block in conjunction with a cuttlebone, or you can use either by itself. A mineral block may also help keep the beak trim.

# Fly, Polly, Fly!: Helping Your Parakeet Get the Exercise She Needs

Wild parakeets fly around all day searching for food and water, and as a result, wild parakeets don't get fat. The companion parakeet, however, is highly prone to obesity. So exercise is essential to maintain your parakeet's good health. And flying is the absolute best exercise for birds. It's the most natural and gives them a sense of purpose. Some people allow their parakeets to fly around the house. Many people build aviaries (bird homes that are large enough for an adult human to fit inside) where their birds can fly.

Many dangers lurk in the common household, and flying in the house may not be the best idea, though some parakeets live out long lives doing just that. (For information on parakeet-proofing your home, see Chapter 4.)

A friendly bird may want to follow you around, and you could accidentally step on him. A parakeet allowed access to the floor may also become victim to a slamming door or another pet. Keep your parakeet off the floor and you eliminate one of the many dangers that threaten this little bird.

A good exercise for parakeets is something you probably haven't considered: *destruction*. Parakeets like to chew — and the more they chew, the more energy they expend. Find toys that your bird likes to fight with and chew, like toys made of soft wood.

Play gyms are another good source of exercise, especially the ones with long ladders attached. Encourage your bird to go up and down the ladder.

The best exercise for your parakeet is to simply get out of the cage and play with you. The more out-of-cage time that your parakeet has, the more exercise he'll get — and the healthier and happier he'll be.

# A Hard Day's Night: Putting Your Parakeet to Bed

Your day is drawing to a close and you're getting ready to go to bed. Although you don't have to read your bird a bedtime story and tuck him in, you have a couple options.

First, you can just turn out the lights and go to sleep. If you follow this simple approach, you can expect your bird to go to sleep too if the room is dark and relatively quiet. If there's a lot of light coming from another room, it may keep the birds up and they may chatter for part of the night. If the room has windows, the birds will definitely be up with the sun.

Many people choose to cover their parakeets at night, which has its advantages. For one, a covered parakeet won't wake up so early in the morning and start chirping. A cover also shuts drafts out of the cage and prevents the birds from disturbances in the night, such as the family cat lurking nearby.

Some parakeets don't like being covered and will thrash around at night. If this is the case, cover only three sides of the cage, giving your bird the opportunity to view the rest of the room.

If the room where your parakeets are housed is very dark, consider a nightlight. Parakeets can become distraught in the darkness if they hear a noise or feel something moving nearby. Your bird will be better off if she can see that the danger is simply someone getting up for a midnight snack.

# Grooming Your Parakeet

You may not have taken grooming into consideration when you bought your parakeet. But just like a dog or a long-haired cat, a parakeet needs some extra, above-and-beyond care to live a long and happy life. In fact, proper and regular grooming is an integral part of good parakeet care.

## Wing clipping

*Wing clipping* is when someone cuts off the ends of the first seven of the ten primary (or flight) feathers of the wing so that the bird won't be able to fly high, but instead will gently flutter to the ground. This practice is common among pet owners and is a painless procedure for the bird — it's equivalent to a human getting a haircut, except that you don't move around with the use of your hair.

Like human hair, flight feathers grow back. You can expect the flight feathers to be back in about five to six months, or after a *molt*, or loss and re-growth of feathers (see the nearby sidebar, "Molting parakeets," for more information). If you want to keep your parakeet's wings clipped, make sure to check the flight feathers every month to make sure none have grown out.

---

## What about the beak?

Most veterinarians recommend that bird owners do *not* trim the beak, and I agree. You can really harm your bird by trimming the beak. If your parakeet's beak seems overgrown, she may have a serious health disorder that needs to be addressed by a veterinarian. The doctor can help your bird with the health problem and trim the beak at the same time.

A healthy bird does things with her beak that will naturally wear it down — eating hard foods, playing with toys, wiping her beak on her perches, and chewing on wood. You can bet that there's a problem if your parakeet's beak needs trimming.

---

### To clip or not to clip

Ah, that is the question! Wing clipping is a much-heated discussion among bird enthusiasts. Some are in favor of clipping and some are against it. Wherever you fall in the argument, you'll have to make a decision about wing clipping. A clipped bird *is* easier to tame, but that doesn't mean that your bird must be clipped for his entire life. Clipping is a very personal decision and you'll have to live with the consequences if something happens to your bird, whether he is clipped or not.

Birds get more exercise and are happier when they can fly. I'd rather take every precaution so that my birds don't get hurt, and keep them fully flighted — but I'm just one voice among many. Ultimately, you need to do what's right for you and your bird.

### How to clip your parakeet's wings

Clipping should allow your parakeet to flutter gently to the floor. If you cut too much, there is the potential for injury. Too little, and the bird could still take off into the wild blue yonder.

Watch someone experienced in clipping, like an avian veterinarian, a breeder, or a bird-shop owner, clip your bird the first time. You won't ever have to clip your bird yourself if you can find someone in your area who will charge you just a few dollars for clipping.

---

# Molting parakeets

*Molting* is when a bird loses some of the old feathers on his body and grows new feathers. When your parakeet is molting, you'll notice more feathers than usual on the floor of the cage, but you shouldn't be able to notice any bald patches or feather loss on the bird himself — if you do, take your bird to the veterinarian right away.

Molting birds are going through a rough, cranky time. Their skin may itch and the new feathers breaking out of their skin may even be painful. This is not the time to try a new training method.

A companion bird may molt once or twice a year, depending on the weather and lighting where you live. Molting is seasonal, but for birds living inside, it can occur any time. Molting can last a few weeks to a few months.

A molting bird will appreciate a daily bath or a spraying. The bath helps to soften the sheathes over the *pin feathers* (the newly grown feathers, also referred to as *blood feathers*) and helps the new feather emerge. Many bird keepers also offer a product called egg food, which you can buy from your local pet store. This product looks like crumbly yellow breadcrumbs and contains a lot of vitamins and minerals that a molting bird needs. Egg food is also good for breeding parakeets.

Clipping a parakeet is a job for two people — one to hold the parakeet gently in a small hand towel and one to clip the wings. The person clipping the wings spreads out the wing carefully, exposing the individual feathers. You'll see the primary flight feathers at the end of the wing, with shorter feathers, the *coverts,* covering the upper part of the flight feathers — never cut these shorter feathers (see Figure 5-2)! Cut the flight feathers parallel to the coverts, about 2 millimeters away from them. Never, *ever* cut into a feather inside a sheath — this is a "living" feather, a blood feather, and will bleed (see the nearby sidebar, "Beware blood feathers"). The sheath looks like thin white plastic covering the rolled-up feather and coming to a point, like a pin (hence, the name *pin feather*), and the material covering it is actually keratin, the same stuff that makes your fingernails.

Only trim feathers in a clean, well-lighted place where you can see what you're doing. If you can't see, you could potentially harm your little bird with those sharp scissors. Always keep a *bird-safe* styptic powder (which you can get at your pet shop or online) on hand in case you accidentally clip a blood feather. Instead of special styptic powder, you can also use baking flour or corn starch, which may be easier on the skin. Styptic powder for human use can burn the skin.

Trim the feathers on both wings evenly. Don't trim only one wing. If the wings are uneven, the parakeet can't control her descent, and she could injure herself trying to land. Some people will advise you to leave the first two primary flight feathers intact, but this isn't a recommended practice — your parakeet could break these feathers easily, because they are no longer protected by the others.

Wing clipping

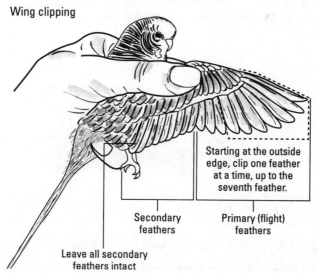

Starting at the outside edge, clip one feather at a time, up to the seventh feather.

Secondary feathers

Primary (flight) feathers

Leave all secondary feathers intact

**Figure 5-2:** For a proper clip, trim the first seven primary flight feathers.

## *Toenail clipping*

Your parakeet may develop sharp little toenails, which will make your relationship with him slightly unpleasant. You don't want to be scratched painfully when you're playing with your bird. Even though your parakeet may have a concrete perch, which is great for keeping the nails trimmed, you may have to manually trim the nails as well.

Your parakeet's nail has two parts, just like your nails do — the dead part of the nail (on the end), and the *quick,* where the blood supply is. Only cut the dead part of the nail, never the quick. Avoiding the quick is easy when you have a parakeet with light-colored nails — you'll be able to see the vein in the nail and avoid it. If you have a bird with dark-colored nails, trim a very tiny amount off the tip of the nail, rather than risk hurting your bird.

Again, as with wing trimming, you'll have to gather your parakeet up in a hand towel. A human nail trimmer works well for your parakeet's little nails, or you can use small dog/cat nail trimmers with a round opening at the clipping end. Keep styptic powder on hand at all times in case of bleeding.

If you make a few passes at your parakeet's nails with a file once a week, the nails will remain trim and you'll eliminate the chances of hurting your bird. Just don't file too much.

With both nails and wings, you're better off clipping less than more — you can always go back and clip more, but you can't take away the fact that you've cut into a blood feather or the quick of a nail (see Figure 5-3).

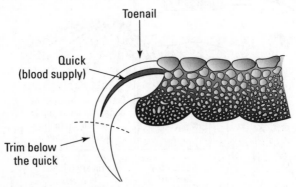

**Figure 5-3:** Try not to cut into the quick when you trim your bird's nails.

# Beware blood feathers

*Blood feathers,* also called *pin feathers,* are newly grown feathers that still have a blood supply and will bleed if they're cut or broken. You can recognize blood feathers by the sheath of material encasing them. If your parakeet is light in color, you may even be able to see a vein inside the feather.

Under no circumstances should you ever cut a blood feather, but if you do, you may have to pull the feather out to stop the bleeding. This advice sounds brutal, I know, but it's actually a commonly practiced method of dealing with broken blood feathers. Simply hold the wing firmly and pull the feather *straight out* with a pair of strong tweezers, *hemostats* (a medical tool used to clamp blood vessels and other things), or small pliers. Do *not* pull the feather out at an angle. Pull swiftly, but don't yank.

If you're too queasy to pull out the broken or cut blood feather yourself, rush to the veterinarian after you've applied a clotting agent to the bleeding area. Even if you've pulled the blood feather yourself, visiting a veterinarian after you've done so is a good idea, just to make sure your bird has no further injury.

## *Bathing your bird*

Parakeets love to bathe, and watching them happily splashing away in a bird bath is a real treat. A shallow dish of tepid water should get your parakeet in the mood to bathe. Many parakeet owners use misters or spray bottles to bathe their birds, while others find that running the faucet in the kitchen sink brings the bird running.

Encourage bathing in the daylight hours so that your bird doesn't go to sleep wet.

You may not think that a bird bathing in winter is a good idea, but it's actually fine. Your home may be very dry in winter and the bird may need to moisten her skin. Birds generally know what's best when it comes to bathing, so trust your parakeet's instincts.

You don't need to blow-dry or towel-dry your parakeet (and blow-drying can be deadly if your blow-dryer has nonstick coating on its coils). Provide a warm lamp for the bird to sidle up to if he's cold. *Remember:* If you provide a lamp, make sure it's not too close! The bird should be able to move at least 18 inches away from it. Healthy birds generally dry pretty quickly anyway, in a half hour or so in most weather.

In your local pet shop, you'll see some bathing products that claim to be good for a bird's skin and feathers. But these products may irritate your parakeet's eyes if you spray the product in them. Read product labels and use your best judgment — or save your money and use good old-fashioned water.

# Parakeets and Other Pets

Your parakeet is in serious danger if a hungry cat or mischievous dog can easily get to him. Cats are death to parakeets — they can never, ever be trained not to want to catch and kill birds. Cats also have a type of bacteria on their nails and teeth that can kill a bird overnight from just a tiny scratch.

Many dogs, like terriers and sight hounds, are bred to want to kill small, swiftly moving objects, which describes your parakeet perfectly. All dogs pose a danger to your bird.

Ferrets and rats will also waste no time hunting and killing your bird. Rabbits, however, pose no danger.

Fish tanks and bowls may be a tempting bathing hole for your parakeet, but they pose a serious drowning threat. Keep all standing water covered.

Other, more aggressive birds are a deadly threat to your parakeet, who is a pretty docile creature by nature. Lovebirds, conures, amazons, cockatoos, macaws, ringnecks, and other aggressive birds should be kept well away from your parakeet. Cockatiels, canaries, and finches are generally more sociable with parakeets.

# Chapter 6

# Come Here Often? Getting to Know Your Parakeet

. . . . . . . . . . . . . . . . . . . . . . . . . . . . . . . . . . . . . . . . . .

*In This Chapter*

▶ Taming and training your parakeet

▶ Dealing with biting

▶ Teaching your parakeet to talk

. . . . . . . . . . . . . . . . . . . . . . . . . . . . . . . . . . . . . . . . . .

*O*ne reason why the parakeet has become the world's favorite bird is because of its behavior. The parakeet is a bundle of energy, affectionate and saucy, and is, in general, pretty predictable. This chapter helps you recognize normal and abnormal parakeet behavior and gives you the basics of taming and training.

## Understanding Parakeet Behavior

Each bird has his own personality, likes, and dislikes, but some behaviors are common to all parakeets. These behaviors include:

✔ **Dancing in front of the cage door.** *Translation:* "Get me outta here!" A parakeet making a commotion in front of the cage door wants to come out and play.

✔ **Head tipped downward, as if in prayer.** *Translation:* "Gimme a little head scratch!" When you're playing with your parakeet and he tips his head toward you, he wants a little preening.

✔ **Backing into a corner, beak open, wings flared.** *Translation:* "Stay back!" This is a bird being territorial at the moment. He may also be frightened.

✔ **Crouched posture, wings fluttering, staring at you.** *Translation:* "Play with me — now!" This posture (see Figure 6-1), especially with the wings fluttering, means that your little Polly is really in love with you!

✔ **Fluffing and shaking.** *Translation:* "I'm sleepy" or "I'm getting ready to do something other than what I'm doing right now." A sleepy parakeet will fluff and shake his feathers a few times before drifting off to sleep. You can liken this to a human tossing and turning a few times before getting completely comfortable. A quick fluff and shake means that the bird is about to embark on a new task.

✔ **Banging toys around.** *Translation:* "I'm sick of being in this cage" or "I'm having amorous feelings that I need to express." Parakeets bang their toys around for many reasons, but these are probably the most common.

**Figure 6-1:** A crouched parakeet usually wants to go somewhere.

In the following sections, I cover many of the behaviors your parakeet will likely show off for you. All these behaviors are completely normal.

## Cleaning and grinding the beak

Your parakeet will likely wipe his beak after he eats, and he may rake his beak across the bars of his cage or on toys. He's just taking care of himself and keeping himself clean. A healthy parakeet will also grind the upper and lower parts of his beak together after he eats or before he falls asleep. This behavior is a tension-reliever for a bird. This grinding isn't meant to trim the beak — it's more a measure of contentment.

## Preening

A healthy bird will sort through his feathers with his beak, making sure they're all in order, cleaning the unruly and ruffled feathers of debris, and creating a neat and orderly appearance. This behavior is known as *preening*.

If your parakeet *isn't* preening herself, she's probably ill — make an appointment with your avian vet to have her checked out. If you notice that your parakeet has become ragged and disheveled looking, with debris attached to her feathers or patches of feathers missing, get her some medical attention right away.

Parakeets in pairs will engage in mutual preening (see Figure 6-2), called *allopreening*. This behavior is convenient for those hard-to-reach places, like the top of the head. It's also part of the bonding process.

**Figure 6-2:** Parakeets who live together may enjoy mutual preening.

# Fluffing and shaking the feathers

When your parakeet is getting ready for a catnap or bedtime, he'll fluff himself and then shake out his feathers a few times, which helps to release energy and gets him comfortable. Parakeets also shake themselves when they get ready to do a new task, such as eat or take a bath, and they always shake after grooming, allowing all the debris they've just picked off to fall away and leave the feathers clean.

If you notice that your parakeet remains fluffed and that he's sleeping for hours on end when he used to be playing, he may be ill.

# Stretching

Your parakeet will perform a kind of daily birdy yoga, stretching all parts of his body. He'll amaze you with the kinds of stretches he can do. He'll lift his leg and his wing, both on the same side at the same time, and do a long, satisfying stretch — very impressive. This type of stretch is called *mantling*.

## Yawning and sneezing

Parakeets yawn and sneeze just as people do. Parakeets yawn for much the same reasons as well — and they pass a yawn onto their pals, just as humans do, too. Parakeets sneeze to clear their nasal passages when they're clogged. Sound familiar?

## Resting on one leg

Your healthy parakeet will often sleep or rest on one leg, which helps to regulate her body temperature.

If you notice that your parakeet is sleeping with both feet on the perch, fluffed up, with her head tucked behind her, she may be ill. Watch for other signs of illness and get her some medical attention if the behavior continues.

## Tucking and bobbing the head

Your parakeet will likely sleep with his head tucked in the fluffed up feathers on his back. This behavior is another example of birdy yoga — it seems an almost impossible position. Although it's completely normal behavior, some birds choose not to sleep this way (just as some people sleep on their sides and others prefer their backs).

Bobbing of the head is normal, too. You'll often see this during feeding behaviors and mating dances.

If the bobbing produces vomit that crusts on the bird's beak and feathers, call your veterinarian.

## Scratching

Parakeets are almost constantly moving and preening — scratching is just part of the parakeet routine. A male parakeet who is feeling amorous (wantin' some birdy lovin') will often prance up and down the perch, scratching at his face. This scratching doesn't mean that your parakeet has lice or mites — it's normal behavior.

If you notice that your parakeet is scratching himself to the point of bleeding or if he's scratching bald patches of skin on his body, take him to an avian veterinarian right away.

## Regurgitating

Believe it or not, your bird bobbing his head and trying to regurgitate his food on you is a sign of intense affection. Regurgitation is how birds feed one another and how they feed their babies. Your parakeet, especially a male, may regurgitate to you, his toys, or his mate. If you notice that he's sitting on the perch (or the bottom of the cage) vomiting onto his chest, the material is sticking to his feathers and face, and he's shaking his head to get it off of him, get veterinary attention right away. No healthy adult parakeet would allow debris to accumulate on his feathers.

Regurgitation and vomiting are different — regurgitation is for affection and to feed mates and babies and vomiting is due to illness.

## Flapping the wings

Sometimes a parakeet will stand on a perch and flap his wings vigorously, like birdy calisthenics. If you see your parakeet doing this, don't be alarmed — he's just exercising, getting rid of some of the energy he has built up in his little system. Even if your parakeet has a very large cage, such as an aviary, he may still flap to his heart's content. Parakeets also flap to loosen their feathers during a molt, to help speed up the process of growing new feathers.

## Playing

Playing comes in many forms — chewing, banging toys around, chasing cage mates, zooming around the aviary, tossing food out of the bowl, anything to remain entertained. Sometimes what looks like aggression, such as violently banging a certain toy against the cage, is just a form of play — nothing to be concerned about.

## Dancing on the perch

Male parakeets do a funny thing I like to call "perch dancing." the male struts up and down the perch, bobbing his head, chattering, and scratching his face. This dance is intended to get the attention of the female, who generally sits there, pretending not to notice. It's a charming little dance, and it's perfectly normal. Your male parakeet may dance to a toy, or even to you, if you're lucky.

## Bathing

Healthy parakeets love to bathe. In warm weather, your parakeet may bathe every day. Your parakeet will probably get completely wet, dunking his breast and face in the water and fluffing the water up over his back. Provide your parakeet with a shallow dish of water every day (not so often in cold weather) and watch the show. *Remember:* If your parakeet likes to bathe in his water dish, make sure you change the water frequently. Parakeets also like to bath in wet greens, such as kale, placed in a dish on top of the cage.

## Getting excited

Parakeet excitement comes in many forms — clambering around the cage, flying, making loud noises, and talking, among others. Sometimes parakeets are excited by certain types of music or by the addition of something new in the home.

## Getting scared

A frightened parakeet may thrash around in his cage, crouch in the corner with his beak wide open, bite, or fly aimlessly around, hitting things in the aviary or home. He may stand tall on his perch, making himself very sleek, and look around agitatedly.

To calm a frightened parakeet, remove the offending item (if you know what it is) and cover the cage for half an hour. This should give the bird time to calm down and assess the situation — he's familiar with the comfort of his cage. After half an hour, you can uncover the front of the cage and give him a millet spray. When he's eaten for a while, remove the entire cover, slowly, and he should be okay.

## Egg laying

Sometime single female parakeets will lay eggs, even without a male around. When the hours of light get longer than the hours of darkness, parakeets will get into breeding mode, often causing the female to lay eggs. This generally happens in the spring or if you leave her light on for more than 12 hours per day for several days in a row.

If your single female lays eggs, let her have them for a few days if she wants them (often she will toss them aside and ignore them), and then remove them from her. Make sure that the light reaches her cage for about ten hours a day, no more. This strategy should calm her hormones.

A hen (female) that's laying eggs needs more calcium and vitamins than usual. Make sure that she has a cuttlebone, and offer her crushed hardboiled eggs, shell and all. Lots of veggies are great for her, too, but avoid spinach, kale, and parsley at this time — all of these contain an acid that binds calcium, making it unusable to the body (for humans as well).

# Handling Your Parakeet Safely

 Parakeets should be handled gently and with respect. Here are some basic ground rules to share with your children when you first bring your parakeet home. **Remember:** These rules also apply to adults. In fact, think of them as ground rules that everyone should follow all the time:

- **Move slowly.** Birds are frightened by quick movements. Explain to children that the bird won't hurt them (not badly, anyway) and that it's important to remain calm, no matter what happens.

- **Speak softly.** Loud noises are terrifying to a parakeet. Use a soft, soothing voice when talking to the bird.

- **Don't fear the bird.** Fear of the new parakeet will lead to an unhappy and neglected bird.

- **Never shake, hit, or rattle the cage.** A parakeet is going to be only as entertaining as he can be. Children don't always understand this — and they try to get the bird to do something more interesting. Explain to children that birds become frightened when their homes are rattled.

- **Allow the bird to play.** Birds need some out-of-cage time every day. With your busy life, you can easily forget that your bird relies on you for interaction. Perhaps the bird can sit on your shoulder while you read, do homework, or watch television.

- **Give the bird a routine.** Birds like to know what will happen and when it will happen. They are control freaks with feathers. Create a parakeet routine for yourself or your child and make sure that you stick with it.

- **Birds need "time out" too.** Parakeets can get overstimulated and tired if they're handled by an active child (or adult) for hours on end. The poor bird will want nothing more than to take a drink of water, eat a snack, and take a nap. The bird needs a break every half hour or so.

- **Never take the parakeet outside.** Kids may want to show off their bird to friends, and though that's a valid response to owning this terrific animal, many dangers lurk outside, including the bird flying away. Even a clipped bird can be carried away by a breeze.

✔ **Don't squeeze!** Birds are unable to breathe when held, even lightly, around their chest area. Don't "carry around" the bird. Instead, let the bird perch on your hand or shoulder.

Always supervise your child's playtime with your parakeet. Children are whimsical and may leave the bird somewhere or may become panicked by a little nip.

# Dealing with Problem Behaviors

Problem behaviors are any behaviors that aren't normal in a *healthy*, well-cared for parakeet. These behaviors are things to look out for because they may indicate illness or unhappiness.

## Feather plucking

Most parakeets will not pluck their feathers the way other, larger parrots do, but self-mutilation is not unheard of in parakeets, especially if a medical condition is affecting the bird. Sometimes, an infection or virus can cause an itchy or painful spot that the bird will pick and make bald and raw.

If you notice that your parakeet is "over-preening," or you see bald spots on your bird, take him to your avian veterinarian right away — there could be a serious underlying cause.

## Night frights

Night frights happen when a parakeet becomes agitated or fearful in the dark and thrashes against the bars of his cage, often causing eye, foot, and feather injury. If you hear thrashing in the night, consider using a nightlight in your parakeet's room or lifting a corner of the cover during the night so that a bit of light gets through.

# Taming and Training Your Parakeet

When it comes to parakeets, taming and training are essentially the same thing. Most people will not spend hours upon hours training their parakeets to do elaborate tricks, nor is your average parakeet going to *do* elaborate tricks. So, for the purpose of this book, I merge taming and training into one seamless method.

## *Helping your parakeet feel comfortable around you*

Begin the taming process about a week to ten days after you bring your new bird home. You have to give your parakeet some time to get acclimated to his new environment, so you don't want to start on the very first day.

Unless you've bought a handfed baby, you can't just fish a parakeet out of his cage, place him on your finger, and expect him to stay there. The untamed parakeet will flutter or fly as far away from you as possible and go to the highest point he can reach.

You can do several things to make this taming time comfortable for him:

✔ Talk in a soothing tone to your new bird, saying his name over and over.

✔ Offer treats, such as millet spray, placing them inside the cage and letting your hand linger inside for a moment.

✔ Place your hand on the side of the cage, very slowly, two or three times a day. Don't expect the bird to come near your finger. You're just getting him used to your hand being near him.

During the taming phase, play hide-and-seek with your parakeet. Hide around a corner and whistle and click to your bird — you'll get him interested in what you're doing. When he whistles or vocalizes back, pop out and greet him.

Talk and sing as much as you can around your parakeet, especially when you're servicing his cage. He'll get used to the sound of your voice and he may even begin calling to you for more vocal interaction.

The key to taming and training a parakeet is trust. Making taming and training fun is the best way to gain your bird's trust. Keeping that in mind, here are some taming and training don'ts:

✔ Don't grab a frightened and thrashing bird out of the cage and whisk her away to another room — you'll just end up scaring your bird even more.

✔ Never, ever wear gloves during taming or training. Gloves will only terrify your parakeet out of his little feathers and he won't get used to the human hand.

✔ Don't yell at or hit your parakeet, ever, ever, *ever*. Those are just not good training tactics (and are considered animal abuse).

✔ Don't get your feelings hurt by a bite — your bird isn't being a jerk; she's just being a bird. ***Remember:*** The more reaction you have when the bird bites you, the more frequently and harder the bird is going to bite. If you're calm and act as if the bite doesn't hurt a bit, the bird will be less likely to bite next time.

The first thing you have to do is build trust with your bird, making each hand-on experience with your parakeet a pleasant one. If each time you play with your parakeet *you* behave in a mature, soothing manner, making yourself a fun and enjoyable companion, you and your parakeet will have a great relationship for many years.

Before you try to tame your parakeet, you need to clip his wings so that he can't fly. Don't worry, the wing feathers grow back. Even if you eventually want your parakeet to be a "flyer," you won't get far in your training if you have an unclipped bird. Your parakeet will be able to get away from you if he can fly — and that doesn't do much for the training process.

## *Showing your bird the way*

After your bird is comfortable around you, you can start trying to train your parakeet. Just keep these suggestions in mind:

✔ Bribe the parakeet with fun foods and toys she likes.

✔ Move slowly and talk in a soothing manner.

✔ Try to read your parakeet's body language. If he's getting terrified or frustrated, put him in his cage for a rest.

✔ Do several short training sessions a day rather than one or two long ones. Shoot for no longer than 10 or 15 minutes.

✔ Have realistic expectations for your parakeet. Training takes time.

An easy behavior to train your parakeet to do is the step-up. *Step-up* is when your bird steps gently on to your hand or finger. Fortunately, your finger is kind of like a perch, and if your finger is always steady and safe, your parakeet will eventually learn to trust you.

Parakeets are fast learners — especially with simple tasks, like step-up. All it takes to teach a parakeet anything is mutual trust and patience. Using a gentle, slow training method is preferable with animals as sensitive as parakeets.

Begin by allowing the bird to come out of his cage by himself or scoop him up gently with a washcloth. Try not to frighten him. Place a perch on top of his cage, or let him climb on to a standing perch where he will be standing on a dowel, not a flat surface. If your parakeet is a tame youngster, you can gently lift him out of the cage, being careful that you don't hurt his feet.

Take the bird to a small room, perhaps a closet or a bathroom, but definitely a place that's parakeet-proofed so that he doesn't get hurt. If you're taking him to the bathroom, put the toilet lid down and remove any cleaning products. (You want to parakeet-proof the room *before* you take the bird out of his cage.)

After you're in the small room, sit down with your knees bent and up. Place the bird on one knee. The idea is to have him stay there so that you can talk to him and offer millet spray, all the while creeping your hand slowly up your leg toward him. In your first few sessions, he'll probably fly off. That's okay — just pick him up and put him back on your knee.

When you have his trust (after a few sessions) and after he's let you get very close with your hand, try to rub his chest and belly softly and gently with the length of your index finger, cooing to him, pushing on his belly, and slowly increasing the pressure.

Increase the pressure on his belly a little more, and he'll lift up a foot to keep his balance. Place your finger or hand under his lifted foot and lift him, if he allows it. If not, simply allow his foot to remain on your hand until he removes it. As you do this, tell him clearly to *step up*. Many parakeets will say "step up" and wave one foot in the air when they want you to pick them up. This command becomes a great communication tool.

When your bird is fairly good at stepping up, you can have him step him from finger to finger, repeating the phrase "step up" and praising him.

# Talking to Your Parakeet — and Getting Him to Talk to You

Parakeets are among the best talking birds, able to mimic hundreds of words and phrases. Males are more likely to talk then females, and some individuals are very chatty, while others won't talk much at all, but females may take to whistling more easily. Whistling is easier for a parakeet to learn, so if you teach whistles before you teach talking, your bird may prefer the whistling and may not talk much. But each parakeet is different in this regard.

The best (and only) way to teach any bird to talk is through repetition. Your bird will say the things that you say all the time. Mine call my dogs, repeat noises and words that they've heard on television (which I keep on for them), and say things back to me that I say to them, like "I love you," "Hello, Polly," and "Good night."

If you want, you can make a recording and play it all day when you're not home. But your parakeet is more likely to learn things that you say in person. He's paying attention to his human family and trying to get their attention and be part of things by talking.

## Talking to your parakeet

Some people use baby talk when they talk to their parakeets, and others talk to them like they are adult humans. Talk to your parakeets whichever way feels natural to you, but realize that you have to speak very clearly if you want your bird to speak clearly as well.

Repeating yourself a lot is the best way to get your bird to say what you want him to say. Most people don't need to make this much effort — a parakeet generally repeats what she hears a lot, usually her name and *hello*. She'll generally also repeat what she hears you saying to other people in the house. If you have naughty kids, your bird may learn to say, "I told you to stop hitting your sister!"

You can teach your parakeet your name and phone number in case he ever gets lost. Many people do this, and it actually does work to return the bird to his family. Simply repeat your name and phone number over and over — you can make a little song of it if you'd like — and the bird may very well pick it up.

## Understanding a duo's behavior

Two parakeets interacting can be really cute if they like each other. They will sit together and preen each other. The male will do a little mating dance, strutting up and down the perch, scratching his face. They will chitter-chatter to each other. These behaviors are all ways in which parakeets communicate.

When parakeets don't like each other, one may chase the other around the cage, not allowing him near the food and water dishes. One may pluck the other one's feathers or nip at his feet. These parakeets should be separated — possibly forever.

# Chapter 7

# Keeping Your Parakeet Healthy and Handling Emergencies

he best defense against illness that a parakeet has is a diligent guardian. Just like you, your parakeet needs a doctor and yearly check-ups. He also needs you to know when he's not feeling well — which means you need to understand the signs he's giving you. Finally, in the rare event of a parakeet emergency, he needs you to get him the help he needs — and fast!

This chapter helps you to become your parakeet's first line of defense against the Grim Reaper.

## The Veterinarian: Your New Best Friend

For your parakeet, you want an *avian veterinarian,* a vet who specializes in the care and treatment of birds.

The best place to find an avian vet in your area is by calling the Association of Avian Veterinarians at 561-393-8901 or visiting www.aav.org.

## Regular examinations

Take your new pet to an avian veterinarian within three days of buying him. Here's why:

- ✔ If you bought your parakeet with a health guarantee, you'll have some recourse if tests reveal that your new bird is ill.

- ✔ You'll begin a relationship with the vet, and the vet will get to know your bird and be able to evaluate him better because the doctor will know what your bird is like when he's healthy.

- ✔ Some avian vets won't take an emergency patient unless the bird is a regular client. You don't want to be stuck without someone to call if your parakeet encounters an emergency.

- ✔ Avian vets often board birds in their offices, though some will only board clients — that way they can be relatively sure that the bird won't bring diseases into their office.

- ✔ You'll get some important recommendations from the doctor, including information on diet and housing.

Even when your parakeet is well, you should take him to your avian veterinarian at least once a year. Your veterinarian will run some routine tests and weigh your bird. This *well-bird check-up* will allow your veterinarian to keep records of your healthy bird and will make it easier to determine when he's ill.

## Emergencies

When you have an emergency involving your parakeet, you *must* take him to an avian veterinarian right away.

So what qualifies as an emergency? If you have *one single moment* of worry about something that has happened to your bird (he's flown into a window, broken a toe, is bleeding, and so on), or if you notice a drastic change in your parakeet's behavior, you probably have an emergency.

Don't hesitate to rush your bird to the avian veterinarian. Minutes are crucial in an emergency. ***Remember:*** Your bird is a small, sensitive creature more likely to be overcome by the stress of an accident than a larger animal.

# What a Healthy Bird Looks Like

Knowing something about the parakeet's bodily systems and observing your bird carefully when he's healthy will help you to be able to tell if he's ill.

## Eyes

A healthy eye is clear, moist, and free of discharge. A parakeet with an eye problem may squint or scratch it excessively with his foot or will rub his eye on the perch or sides of his cage.

If you see swollen eyelids, cloudy eyes, excessive blinking or discharge, and tearing, have your bird checked out by your vet.

## Ears

Your parakeet's ears are located a short distance parallel from the eyes and look like holes in the head. Each ear opening is covered by feathers. You may get a glimpse of the ear openings after your parakeet bathes, when the feathers around his head are wet and stuck together.

If you can see your parakeet's ear opening without the bird being wet, make an appointment with your avian veterinarian.

## Beak

Your parakeet's beak is made of the same durable material as your fingernails. The beak grows over a basically hollow honeycomb-like structure, a convenient design for an animal that should be light enough to fly. The beak acts as a crushing tool but is delicate enough to peel the skin off a pea. The beak also helps your parakeet around, kind of like another foot.

Your parakeet should be able to keep his beak trim through eating and playing. If your bird's beak is overgrown (see Figure 7-1), it could be an indication of a nutritional disorder or mites, and you'll have to take him to an avian veterinarian for treatment.

Never try to trim your parakeet's beak yourself.

The *cere,* the fleshy place just above the beak, can sometimes become thick and rough in *hens* (female birds), a condition called *brown hypertrophy.* This condition, though not serious, is likely caused by hormones and should be treated by a veterinarian.

**Figure 7-1:** An overgrown beak may be a sign of malnutrition or mites.

# Feet

In addition to walking and climbing, birds also use their feet to regulate their body temperature. When your parakeet is cold, he may draw one leg up into his body and stand on the other leg. When your parakeet is warm, the blood flow will increase to his legs, which will help his whole body cool down.

Several injuries are common to the feet, including catching toes on cages and toys, as well as problems with the leg band. Swelling in the legs could be a symptom of *gout* (a painful condition that can be the result of poor nutrition). If the skin on the bottom of the foot is red and inflamed, or even scabby, this could be a sign of *bumblefoot* (an infection associated with poor nutrition and obesity).

If you notice something wrong with your bird's legs or feet, take him to your avian vet. Contact your avian veterinarian right away if you notice any foot or leg weakness or *lameness* (inability to walk).

# Feathers

A healthy parakeet should be obsessed with taking care of his feathers, preening them for much of the day. A parakeet likes to keep his feathers neat, clean, and well organized on his body.

Preening keeps the feathers neat and distributes oil through the feathers. The oil, which comes from a gland located on the base of the tail, helps to keep the feathers waterproof and the skin healthy.

Birds *molt* (shed their feathers and grow new ones) once or twice a year, usually during seasonal changes. When your parakeet molts, you'll notice feathers on the bottom of the cage, but you shouldn't be able to see patches of skin on your bird. (If you do notice bald spots, contact your vet — it could indicate a serious medical problem.)

When a new feather begins growing, it will be encased in a protective sheath called a *pin feather.* Pin feathers can be itchy and your parakeet may become cranky at this time, not wanting to be played with as often.

Occasionally, unhappy or ill parakeets will pick and pluck at their feathers. If the problem is medical or nutritional, an avian veterinarian may be able to help solve the problem. If the problem is psychological, you may have to be more diligent in caring for your bird and keeping him happy. Birds confined or kept in stressful situations may pick themselves in order to relieve the stress or boredom. Provide your bird with enough space and toys, and if the behavior continues, take a trip to the veterinarian.

## Respiratory system

Parakeets have a very sensitive respiratory system, which is sensitive to airborne irritants, such as aerosol sprays, fumes from heated nonstick cookware, and tobacco smoke. They are prone to respiratory illness and distress because their system is more complicated than ours.

If you notice your parakeet panting, call your avian veterinarian and describe the situation. Keep your parakeet away from fumes and airborne toxins.

If you notice a change in your bird's breathing or, in extreme cases, bubbling from the mouth or nostrils, take your parakeet to the veterinarian right away. Your parakeet could have a respiratory infection.

## Skeletal system

Many of your parakeet's bones are filled with air, and all of them are thin-walled, which makes them light enough for flight. Though bird bones are strong enough to allow the movement of wings in flight, they're easily broken.

If you suspect that one of your parakeet's bones is broken, take him to the veterinarian immediately. Some of the bones contain air sacs that aid in breathing, and your bird may experience respiratory problems if he has broken bones. Symptoms should be relatively obvious — if you see your bird with a leg hanging, a wing hanging, or the bird goes lame, it could indicate a break. Of course, if you see a break (as you would in a human), you'll know right away.

## Digestive system

The parakeet's digestive system begins with the beak and ends with the vent. After your bird swallows food, the food goes to the *crop* near the bird's breast. From the crop, the food goes to the stomach then on to the gizzard, which grinds the food. Then the food moves on to the *cloaca,* where the feces, *urates* (the off-white or yellowish opaque part of the dropping), and urine collect before being eliminated through the *vent.*

Because your parakeet will probably be munching all day, she'll be pooping all day too. This is normal. Frequent pooping is a function of flying — a bird that's holding a load of poop is going to be heavier, so nature gave birds a smaller area to hold waste, so it has to be eliminated often.

Poop should have three parts to it — a green semisolid part, a yellowish-white part (urates), and a watery part (urine). Sometimes the color of the poop changes according to what you're feeding your bird. If you feed blueberries or beets, for example, expect the color to change. If you feed greens, expect there to be more urine in the feces — this is normal and isn't considered diarrhea.

If you notice a drastic change in your bird's droppings, see your avian veterinarian.

One common digestive disorder comes from feeding grit to parakeets. Parrots don't need grit the way other types of bird may. If your parakeet eats too much grit, it can stay in the crop and cause impaction. The crop will not be able to empty, and will become distended. You may notice bloody feces with undigested seeds in it.

Ever wonder why your parakeet poops so often? Birds who fly have to stay light, and eliminating droppings frequently is one way of doing just that.

# Signs and Symptoms of a Sick Parakeet

Any odd behavior may indicate illness, but not always. Parakeets, like most birds, are creatures of routine, and a sudden break in routine signals that you should investigate your bird's condition.

If you can't find any reason for the unusual behavior, start looking for symptoms of illness, including the following:

- **Fluffiness:** If you notice that your parakeet is overly fluffy, he may be trying to retain heat.

- **Sleepiness:** A sick parakeet may sleep too much. Sleeping on the bottom of the cage is especially telling.

- **Loss of appetite:** If you notice that your bird isn't eating, he could have a serious problem.

- **Weight loss:** This symptom may indicate a number of illnesses.

- **Change in attitude:** If your parakeet seems listless and is not behaving in his usual manner, he may be ill.

- **Change in feathers:** Lack of grooming and feathers falling out in patches can indicate illness.

- **Lameness:** If your bird can't use his feet, you can be guaranteed that something is wrong. Take your bird to the vet right away.

- **Panting or labored breathing:** Either of these symptoms can indicate a respiratory ailment, or perhaps overheating. Changes in your parakeet's breathing, changes in vocalization, or gasping or wheezing can indicate an infection. Panting may also be a sign of egg binding in a female parakeet (see the "Egg binding" section later in this chapter.)

- **Tail bobbing:** If your parakeet is standing straight up on the perch and his tail is noticeably bobbing toward and away from him, he may have a respiratory problem, or he may just be out of breath.

- **Listlessness:** A formerly active parakeet who has become listless and uninterested in life may be ill.

- **Discharge:** If you notice any runniness or discharge on the eyes, nostrils, or vent, go to the veterinarian immediately.

- **Food stuck to the feathers around the face:** This indicates poor grooming or vomiting — possible signs of illness.

- ✔ **Tumors:** Obese parakeets often develop fatty tumors, which may go away with exercise, or may need surgery. Tumors can cause the skin to ulcerate and bleed, and will greatly reduce your parakeet's lifespan.

- ✔ **Change in beak appearance:** A change in the appearance of the beak can indicant scaly-face mites. These occur in young parakeets and older birds with compromised immune systems. These mites cause a crusty appearance on the bird's face and legs, and can result in an overgrown beak. They are easy to treat, but take multiple treatments. Scaly-face mites are not very contagious, but can be passed from bird to bird, so keep infected birds away from others.

- ✔ **Sticky substance in mouth or white mouth lesions:** This can be a sign of a yeast infection, which can affect the mouth and digestive tract, as well as the respiratory system. Your parakeet normally has a certain amount of yeast in its body, but when his bodily balance is out a whack, when he is undernourished or after a treatment of antibiotics, the fungus can grow to excess. Regurgitation and digestive problems may also occur. Even though this condition is not immediately serious, it can cause death if left untreated.

- ✔ **Abnormal feather growth or feather loss:** If you notice changes in your parakeet's feathers, beyond the normal molting, consult your veterinarian. It may be a symptom of a serious disease that may even be contagious to your other birds and could result in death.

- ✔ **Drastic change in droppings:** Your parakeet's droppings should consist of a solid green portion, white urates (on top of the green), and a clear liquid. If any of these are discolored (darker green, black, yellow, or red) and there has been no change in diet, your bird may have a problem.

# Emergencies: Knowing When to Get Help Immediately

The average home offers plenty of dangers for a parakeet. Even the most careful of owners may encounter an accident with her birds.

When an accident happens, the first thing to do is contact your avian veterinarian. *Never* underestimate an emergency. If you notice weakness, a fluffed appearance, quick breathing, droopy eyes, the inability to perch, or your bird lying on the floor of the cage, rush your parakeet to the veterinarian right away.

In the following sections, I cover the more common emergencies. *Remember:* This list doesn't include everything that could happen to your bird, so if you notice something that doesn't seem quite right, don't be afraid to take your bird to the vet and have him checked out.

## Poisoning

Poisoning generally happens when a parakeet gets into a household product. Ingestion or breathing in the poison are the most common ways a parakeet can become poisoned. Aerosol sprays and other products that leave a fine mist in the air can be particularly harmful for your little bird. Scented candles and plug-in air fresheners may seem harmless, but they can actually cause your parakeet respiratory distress. Even candle "beads" that are unlit can seem like neat pellets to your parakeet — and they can be deadly when ingested. Things like fertilizers, cleansers, and toxic houseplants are deadly, too. Keep your bird away from *all* household products.

Symptoms of poisoning can include vomiting, paralysis, bleeding from the eyes, nose, mouth, or vent, seizures, and shock.

If you suspect that your bird has been poisoned, call the Animal Poison Control Center 24-hour poison hotline at 888-426-4435 (to pay by credit card) or 900-680-0000 (to have the charge automatically added to your phone bill). Rushing to your avian veterinarian is essential to saving your bird's life, though quick response from you with the help of the Animal Poison Control Center can be crucial.

## Animal bites

Animals of all kinds, including your friendly cat, are a danger to parakeets.

When a dog or a cat bites a parakeet, the wound, no matter how small, can be deadly in a matter of hours. Other animals, including humans, have bacteria in their mouths that can cause a deadly infection in a bird.

Even if your other pet was "just playing" with the bird, you should rush to the avian veterinarian right away. In the minutes before you take your bird to the veterinarian, flush a small wound, if you see one, with ⅔ water and ⅓ hydrogen peroxide. If the wound is large, leave it alone and let your veterinarian take care of it.

## Making a hospital cage

If your parakeet becomes injured or ill, put him in a safe, warm spot where he can't hurt himself further and where he can retain his body temperature, like a hospital cage. Making a hospital cage is easy. You'll need a 10-gallon aquarium, an aquarium thermometer, a heating pad, a screen top for the aquarium, paper towels, and a towel.

Put the heating pad on the medium setting and place it underneath one half of the aquarium. Place a few layers of paper towels on the bottom of the aquarium. Put shallow dishes of food and water in the aquarium, too — just make sure the water is very shallow, because a weak bird can drown in water as deep as 2 inches. Place the bird in the aquarium; then cover the aquarium with the screen top. Cover the aquarium three-fourths of the way with a dark towel. The bird should be able to move away from the heat if he wants to. Make sure that the temperature in the tank stays at about 98° to 99° F (about 37° C).

## *Overheating*

If your parakeet is panting, holding his wings out, standing on two feet, or is even lying on the floor of the cage, he may be overcome with heat.

Keep a spray bottle handy and lightly mist your parakeet with cool water, repeating until he's soaked. Watch him closely until his behavior seems normal again. Make sure that he has cool water to drink at all times.

Parakeets should never be kept in full sunlight unless they have a shady spot to retreat to.

If your bird does not respond to misting, remove him from the spot immediately and place him in a cooler environment. If you have a small fan, place the flow of air so that it hits just beside the cage, not directly on it, and mist him again. Put drops of cool water in his beak if he's unable to drink. Call your avian veterinarian.

## *Oil on the feathers*

Oil on the feathers makes it difficult for a parakeet to regulate his body temperature, which can be deadly for a bird. The parakeet may also preen his feathers and ingest this oil, leading to medical problems. How does a parakeet get oil on his feathers? Believe it or not, parakeets occasionally fly into a pot of oil (cool oil, you hope!) or may even find themselves in the middle of an oily salad.

If your bird soaks himself in oil and is otherwise uninjured (the oil was cool), dust him with cornstarch or flour (any kind except gritty corn flour), making sure to keep the flour away from his face. Remove the excess flour with a paper towel. Fill a small tub with warm water and add some grease-fighting liquid dish soap. Gently place the bird in the tub and allow him to soak. You may have to repeat this a few times. Do not scrub! Rinse him using the same method (without the soap), blot him dry, and place him in a hospital cage with a heating pad underneath half of it and most of the top covered. Don't restrict the flow of air, but keep the heat in. Use a thermometer and make sure the cage is between 80° and 90° F (26° and 32° C). Then get him to your avian veterinarian.

## Frostbite

 Frostbite can cause the loss of toes and feet and may even result in death. If you keep your parakeet outdoors during the cold season, consider bringing him inside as a preventative on the coldest nights. A parakeet will hold a frostbitten foot as if it were fractured (frostbite is a painful condition). The frostbitten area will die and turn a dark color.

 If you find the condition early, place your bird in a hospital cage with a 90° F (32° C) temperature and call the veterinarian. If you catch the condition at the point where the affected area has already turned dark, get your bird to the avian veterinarian right away.

## Unconsciousness

A bird may be unconscious for many reasons, but one strong possibility is that something is poisoning the air. If you find your bird unconscious, ventilate the room thoroughly and remove the bird from the area. Call your avian veterinarian immediately. If you're sure that there is no problem in the air, you can try to rouse your parakeet by gently handling him and trying to wake him. Get to your avian veterinarian right away.

## Egg binding

A swollen abdomen may be a sign of egg binding in a female parakeet. If a hen is not well nourished, especially if she hasn't gotten enough calcium in her diet, her eggs may have soft shells, which will make the eggs difficult to lay, resulting in egg binding. Egg binding can also occur when the egg is malformed, or when the bird has a tumor or other disorder of the reproductive system. Symptoms of egg binding include panting and lameness. Consult your veterinarian immediately if you suspect this problem.

Normally, an egg is passed within a day of noticeable swelling. If you notice that your hen is having serious troubles and it's the middle of the night or you can't get to your avian veterinarian right away, move her to a warm (85° F to 90° F, or 29° C to 32° C) and humid hospital cage (see the sidebar earlier in this chapter for tips on making such a cage). Put a few drops of mineral oil or olive oil in her beak with an eye dropper and place a few drops of the same in her vent (where the egg comes out). This may help her to pass the egg.

Even if she does pass the egg, take her to the veterinarian as soon as you can.

## Foot injuries

Don't try to correct a serious foot injury. Place the injured bird in a hospital cage and take him to the vet immediately.

## Eye injuries

If your parakeet's eye has come in contact with an irritant or poison, wash the eye out with saline solution before you take him to the veterinarian. If the injury is from a bite or other type of wound, place the bird in hospital cage until you can get to the veterinarian.

## Seizures

A bird having seizures is in serious condition. Place him in a hospital cage and get to the veterinarian right away. If he comes out of the seizure, you may want to give him a few drops of sugar water to put some electrolytes and sugars into his bloodstream.

## Injury to the beak

Often, injuries to the beak can be fixed by a veterinarian, or the beak will heal itself by growing back. If your parakeet has injured his beak, place the bird in a hospital cage and take him to see the vet.

## Fractures

Do not try to set a fracture by yourself. If you suspect a fracture, get your parakeet to the veterinarian right away. A serious break can lead to serious complications, especially if it occurs in one of the bones containing an air sac.

## When your parakeet breaks the skin (on your finger)

To my knowledge, no one has ever died or gotten ill from a parakeet bite. Sure, parakeets are able to transmit diseases to humans, but not from biting them — I'd be a goner long ago if that were the case. Birds don't have wet mouths like mammals do, so the chances of transmitting disease through a bite are less.

You can treat a bird bite much like you'd treat any other small wound: Use an antiseptic to clean it out, put on some ointment, and apply a bandage. If you want to see your doctor for a bite, go ahead — but you may have to visit often until your parakeet is tamed!

# Assembling a First-Aid Kit

You may be in the position to treat a very minor injury yourself or at least get it under control before you take your bird to your avian veterinarian.

Even though you'll be well equipped with your first-aid kit, it can't take the place of care by your avian veterinarian.

Your birdy first-aid kit should include:

- ✔ Alcohol (for cleaning your tools)

- ✔ Antibiotic ointment (a non-greasy kind, for dressing small wounds)

- ✔ Baby bird formula (for feeding babies or weak adults)

- ✔ Bandages and gauze (for dressing small wounds)

- ✔ Bird-safe styptic powder (to stop bleeding)

- ✔ Bottled water (for cleaning eyes or wounds)

- ✔ Cotton balls (for cleaning small wounds)

- ✔ Dishwashing detergent (mild, for cleaning tools)

- ✔ Eyedropper (for feeding weak birds)

- ✔ Eye wash (for rinsing eyes)

- ✔ Heating pad (for hospital cage)

- ✔ Hydrogen peroxide (for cleaning small wounds)

- ✔ Nail clippers (for clipping nails)

- ✔ Nail file (for filing nails)

- ✔ Pedialyte (to give to weak adult birds)

- ✔ Penlight (to see better)

- ✔ Q-Tips (for cleaning small wounds)

- ✔ Saline solution (for rinsing small wounds or eyes)

- ✔ Sanitary wipes (for your hands)

- ✔ Spray bottle (for spraying solutions onto wounds or eyes)

- ✔ Syringe (without needle, for feeding weak birds)

- ✔ Towels (small, to hold bird)

- ✔ Transport cage (to go to the avian veterinarian)

- ✔ Tweezers (for whatever comes up)

- ✔ Veterinarian's phone number (so you can call in an emergency)

Never give your parakeet any over-the-counter medication meant for humans or other animals. Instead of trying to help the bird yourself, take him to an avian veterinarian immediately.

# Ten Facts About Parakeets

✔ **A female parakeet usually lays four to six eggs per clutch (a** *clutch* **is a group of eggs and then babies when they hatch) but can lay as many as eight to ten eggs.**
It takes the eggs 18 to 20 days to hatch.

✔ **Parakeets can learn to talk as early as 3 months of age.**
Males speak better than females, but certain females talk as well.

✔ **Parakeets have been recorded speaking 600 to 800 words!**
Other parrots, even good talkers, may learn half of that or far, far less. Some larger parrots may learn only a few words or not talk at all.

✔ **When a parakeet bites, it's usually because the bird is afraid or defending his territory or his mate.**
But he could also be defending a toy or something else he's attached to. Most of the time, he's biting because you're trying to catch or restrain him.

✔ **Parakeets can't be** *hybridized,* **or crossed, with another type of bird.**
Other birds, like conures or macaws, will breed regardless of species.

✔ **The average parakeet can live 15 years or longer if taken care of properly.**
Most parakeets will live to be about 7, but you can extend the lifespan of your bird with good nutrition and exercise.

✔ **In the wild, parakeets often flock in large numbers.**
They've been seen in flocks of more than 20,000 to 30,000 birds.

✔ **Myth has it that** *albino* **parakeets (which are white with red eyes) are blind — but this is not the case.**
Albinos can see as well as their pigmented cousins.

✔ **The** *crested parakeet* **is a mutation of the normally feathered parakeet.**
He has a Ringo Starr mop "hairdo" on top of his head. Very cute!

✔ **Parakeets like company.**
They can be kept in a large aviary with zebra finches, cockatiels, and Bourke's parakeets, all of which are also from Australia.

# Ten Fun and Informative Parakeet and Bird Web Sites

- ✔ **American Budgerigar Society** (www.abs1.org)
  This is a great source of information about keeping, breeding, and exhibiting parakeets.

- ✔ **Budgerigar Association of America** (www.budgerigar association.com)
  This is the Web site of the publisher of *Budgerigar Journal Magazine.*

- ✔ **World Budgerigar Organization** (www.worldbudgerigar.org)
  This organization supports and encourages the free movement of budgerigar breeders and budgerigars across international borders in order to improve the breeding, exhibiting, and judging of budgerigars.

- ✔ *Budgerigar World* (www.tuxford.dabsol.co.uk)
  This site is the "Internet portal" for those interested in exhibition budgies. It has lots of great articles and information.

- ✔ **Budgies Galore** (www.budgerigars.co.uk)
  This site contains a wealth of information in articles from some of the top budgerigar breeders and exhibitors in the world.

- ✔ **International Aviculturists Society** (www.funnyfarm exotics.com/IAS)
  This is the Web site of the International Aviculturists Society (IAS), which offers information on keeping and breeding birds and sponsors education programs, breeding programs, and research and conservation.

- ✔ **Budgie Madness** (www.geocities.com/Heartland/3749/index.html)
  This is a fun site dedicated to parakeets.

- ✔ **The World of Budgerigars** (www.budgerigar-world.com/default_I.htm)
  This is a site where all the budgerigar fancies can show photos of their birds and exchange tips and information.

- ✔ **Budgie World** (www.budgieworld.net)
  This site offers lots of great information about budgies plus product suggestions.

- ✔ **Petco** (www.petco.com)
  The Petco Web site offers products, supplies, and accessories your parakeet will love.

# Index

# FOR DUMMIES

## Pet care essentials in plain English

# DOG BREEDS

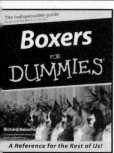
**Boxers For Dummies**
0-7645-5285-6

**German Shepherds For Dummies**
0-7645-5280-5

**Golden Retrievers For Dummies**
0-7645-5267-8

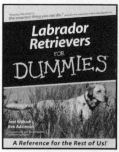
**Labrador Retrievers For Dummies**
0-7645-5281-3

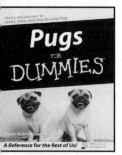
**Pugs For Dummies**
0-7645-54076-9

**Retired Racing Greyhounds For Dummies**
0-7645-5276-7

**Siberian Huskies For Dummies**
0-7645-5279-1

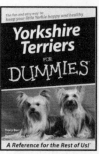
**Yorkshire Terriers For Dummies**
0-7645-6880-9

### Also available:

Jack Russell Terriers For Dummies
(0-7645-5268-6)

Rottweilers For Dummies
(0-7645-5271-6)

Chihuahuas For Dummies
(0-7645-5284-8)

Dachshunds For Dummies
(0-7645-5289-9)

Pit Bulls For Dummies
(0-7645-5291-0)

# DOG CARE, HEALTH, TRAINING, & BEHAVIOR

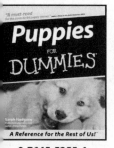
**Puppies For Dummies**
0-7645-5255-4

**Dog Training For Dummies**
0-7645-5286-4

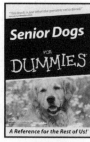
**Senior Dogs For Dummies**
0-7645-5818-8

### Also available:

Choosing a Dog For Dummies
(0-7645-5310-0)

Dog Health & Nutrition For Dummies
(0-7645-5318-6)

Dog Tricks For Dummies
(0-7645-5287-2)

House Training For Dummies
(0-7645-5349-6)

Dogs For Dummies, 2nd Edition
(0-7645-5274-0)

# FOR DUMMIES®

## Pet care essentials in plain English

### CATS & KITTENS

0-7645-5275-9

0-7645-4150-1

### BIRDS

0-7645-5139-6

0-7645-5311-9

### AMPHIBIANS & REPTILES

0-7645-2569-7

0-7645-5313-5

0-7645-5260-0

### FISH & AQUARIUMS

0-7645-5156-6

0-7645-5340-2

### SMALL ANIMALS

0-7645-5259-7

0-7645-0861-X